CZESLAW MILOSZ

Roa

Road-side Dog

Road-side Dog

CZESLAW MILOSZ

TRANSLATED BY THE AUTHOR AND ROBERT HASS

Farrar, Straus and Giroux / New York

Farrar, Straus and Giroux
19 Union Square West, New York 10003

Copyright © 1998 by Czeslaw Milosz
All rights reserved
Distributed in Canada by Douglas & McIntyre Ltd.
Printed in the United States of America
Designed by Abby Kagan
First published in 1997 by Znak, Poland, as Piesek przydrozny
First published in the United States in 1998 by Farrar, Straus and Giroux
First Farrar, Straus and Giroux paperback edition, 1999

Library of Congress Cataloging-in-Publication Data
Milosz, Czeslaw.
    [Piesek przydrozny. English]
    A roadside dog / Czeslaw Milosz
        p.   cm.
    ISBN 0-374-52623-0 (pbk.)
    PG7158.M553P5413   1998
    891.8'58709—dc21   *98-14026*

CONTENTS

ROAD-SIDE DOG

SUBJECTS TO LET

Cogito, sum: certum est quia impossibile . . .
I think I am: it is certain, because it is impossible.

> —*Lew Shestov corrected in this way*
> *Descartes'* cogito ergo sum, *as is*
> *related by Benjamin Fondane in his*
> *book on conversations with Shestov*

Perhaps truth by its nature makes communication between
people impossible, in any case communication by the
intermediary of words. Every one may know it for himself, but
in order to enter into relations with his fellowmen he must
renounce truth and adopt any conventional lie.

> —*Shestov*
> Penultimate Words, *1911*

Road-side Dog

ROAD-SIDE DOG

I went on a journey in order to acquaint myself with my province, in a two-horse wagon with a lot of fodder and a tin bucket rattling in the back. The bucket was required for the horses to drink from. I traveled through a country of hills and pine groves that gave way to woodlands, where swirls of smoke hovered over the roofs of houses, as if they were on fire, for they were chimneyless cabins; I crossed districts of fields and lakes. It was so interesting to be moving, to give the horses their rein, and wait until, in the next valley, a village slowly appeared, or a park with the white spot of a manor in it. And always we were barked at by a dog, assiduous in its duty. That was the beginning of the century; this is its end. I have been thinking not only of the people who lived there once but also of the generations of dogs accompanying them in their everyday bustle, and one night—I don't know where it came from—in a pre-dawn sleep, that funny and tender phrase composed itself: a road-side dog.

NARROW-MINDED

My knowledge is limited, my mind puny. I tried hard, I studied, I read many books. And nothing. In my home, books spill from the shelves; they lie in piles on furniture, on the floor, barring passage from room to room. I cannot, of course, read them all, yet my wolfish eyes constantly crave new titles. In truth, my feeling of limitation is not permanent. Only from time to time an awareness flares of how narrow our imagination is, as if the bones of our skull were too thick and did not allow the mind to take hold of what should be its domain. I should know everything that's happening at this moment, at every point on the earth. I should be able to penetrate the thoughts of my contemporaries and of people who lived a few generations ago, and two thousand and eight thousand years ago. I should. So what?

EYES

Operator: That's how it is. I allowed you, for a moment, to see the bloom of the nasturtium with the eyes of a butterfly. I allowed you to look at a meadow with the eyes of a salamander. Then I gave you the eyes of various people, so that you could look with them at the same city.

—I admit that I was too sure of myself. I admit that there is little similarity between what those streets meant to me and what they were for others walking the same sidewalks I did. If only I were convinced that that was all there was to it—a huge number of individual, uncoordinated perceptions and images. But I have been searching for one, humanly seen, common-to-us-all truth about things, and that's why what you have shown me was such a trial and such a temptation.

WITHOUT CONTROL

He could not control his thoughts. They wandered wherever they liked, and as he observed them, he grew uneasy. For they were not good thoughts, and if he were to judge himself by them, there was, deep within him, a lot of cruelty. He thought that the world was very painful and that human beings didn't deserve to exist. And he suspected that the cruelty of his imagination was somehow connected with his creative impulse.

A SEARCH

A feeling that there must be a set of words in which the essence, so to speak, of the horror discovered in this century could be captured. Readings in memoirs, reminiscences, reports, novels, poems, always with hope and always with the same result: "Not quite." Only timidly did the thought emerge that the truth about the fate of man on earth is different from the one we were taught. Yet we recoil from giving it a name.

NOT MINE

All my life to pretend this world of theirs is mine
And to know such pretending is disgraceful.
But what can I do? Suppose I suddenly screamed
And started to prophesy. No one would hear me.
Their screens and microphones are not for that.
Others like me wander the streets
And talk to themselves. Sleep on benches in parks,
Or on pavement in alleys. For there aren't enough prisons
To lock up all the poor. I smile and keep quiet.
They won't get me now.
To feast with the chosen—that I do well.

THE LAST JUDGMENT

The consequences of our actions. Completely unknown, for every one of them enters into a multifaceted relation with circumstance and with the actions of others. An absolutely efficient computer could show us, with a correction for accidents, of course, for how else to calculate the direction taken by a billiard ball after it strikes another? Besides, it is permissible to maintain that nothing happens by accident. Be that as it may, standing before a perfectly computerized balance sheet of our lives (The Last Judgment), we must be astonished: Can it be that I am responsible for so much evil done against my will? And here, on the other scale, so much good I did not intend and of which I was not aware?

ANIMA

He was writing more and more about women. Did it mean that his anima, oppressed for years, asked, late, for liberation? Or, to put it differently, that his subconscious, until then liberating itself only in his poems, took upon itself the role of a gentle woman physician who had to strip him of his armor before touching his flesh?

OLD PEOPLE

The view of old and ugly men and women, especially of those crones shuffling along with their canes. They were betrayed by their bodies, once beautiful and ready to dance. Yet in every one a lamp of consciousness is burning, hence their wonder: "Is this me? But it can't be so!"

IS AWARENESS SUFFICIENT?

There was a time when it seemed to me that it would be enough to be aware to avoid repetition; i.e., to avoid the fate of other mortals. What nonsense. And yet the separation of the body from consciousness, assigning a magic power to consciousness—that it was enough to *know* and the spell would be broken—that was not so stupid.

IN THE PLACE OF THE CREATOR

Had you been given the power to create the world anew, you would have thought and thought, only to come at last to the conclusion that it would be impossible to conceive anything better than what exists. Take a seat in a café and look at the men and women passing by. Agreed, they could have been beings with immaterial bodies, not subject to the passing of time, to illness and death. Yet precisely the infinite richness, complexity, many-shapedness of earthly things comes from their being self-contradictory. The mind would have been without grace had it not been anchored in matter: slaughterhouses, hospitals, cemeteries, pornographic films. And our physiological necessities would have stifled us with their animal dullness, if not for the playful mind, cut loose, frolicking above. And the guide of consciousness, irony, could not have exercised in its beloved occupation, spying on the flesh. It looks as if the Creator, whose ethical motives people have learned to doubt, was prompted primarily by his desire to make everything as interesting as possible, and as comic.

MEANWHILE AND MAKE-BELIEVE

To get up in the morning and go to work, to be bound to people by the ties of love, friendship, or opposition—and all the time to realize that it was only meanwhile and make-believe. For in him hope only was permanent and real, so strong that he was impatient with living. He was to catch now, in a minute—to catch what? A magic formula which contains all the truth about existence. He would brush his teeth and it was just there, he would take a shower and practically pronounce it, had he not taken a bus, it would have revealed itself, and so on all day long. Waking up at night, he felt he was working his way toward it through a thin curtain, but then, in that striving, he would fall asleep.

He did not regard kindly this affliction of his. He agreed with the opinion that he should be here—entirely present, in a given place and moment, attentive to the needs of those who were close to him and fulfilling their expectations. To think that they were just for meanwhile and that he practiced with them a make-believe was to harm them, yet he was unable to renounce the thought that, really, he had no time for life with them.

EMBARRASSING

Poetry is an embarrassing affair; it is born too near to the functions we call intimate.

Poetry cannot be separated from awareness of our body. It soars above it, immaterial and at the same time captive, and is a reason for our uneasiness, for it pretends to belong to a separate zone, of spirit.

I was ashamed of being a poet, as if, undressed, I would display in public my physical defects. I envied people who do not write poems and whom for that reason I ranged among the normal. And in this I was wrong: few of them deserve to be called that.

FEELING FROM INSIDE

In the act of writing, a transformation occurs: the direct data of consciousness, our feeling of ourselves from inside, is changed into an image of other individuals, similarly feeling themselves from inside, and thanks to that, we can write about them, not only about ourselves.

TO SING GODS AND HEROES

The difference between the kind of poetry in which an "I" tells about itself and a poetry which "sings gods and heroes" is not great, since in both cases the object of description is mythologized. And yet . . .

GRATEFUL

I am grateful for that day when in a wooden little church between huge oaks I was admitted to the Roman Catholic Church. As well for my long life, so that, believing or not believing, I could meditate on two thousand years of my history.

That history was diabolic, no less than heavenly. We built cities bigger than Jerusalem, Rome, and Alexandria. Our ships circumnavigated oceans. Our theologians contrived syllogisms. And immediately the transformation of the planet Earth began. If only we were innocent, but no. No innocence in the expeditions of the cross and the sword.

ACTS AND GRACE

Undoubtedly, the hope of Salvation has paled and now it is so weakened that no images are associated with it. Therefore, even when you tell yourself, "If you want to save your soul, you should renounce things which are the most precious to you, your creative work, a romance, power, or other satisfactions of your ambitions," it is so hard to accomplish this. Once, when Salvation signified a palm in Heaven, and damnation, eternal tortures in the abysses of Hell, people, it seems, had a stronger incitement to search for saintliness and to temper their gluttonous appetites. Not at all. They killed, committed adultery, grabbed the land of their neighbor, and were avid for fame. Something is wrong here. The tangible presence of Paradise, as promised to the Islamic faithful who fell in battle against the infidel, may increase their fervor in combat, but, in general, life on earth and the idea of Salvation seem to belong to two different orders, hardly connected.

It is not improbable that Martin Luther guessed this when he made Salvation dependent not upon acts but upon Grace.

"The poet Jean Valentine once said in an interview, 'Of course all poetry is prayer. Who else would we be addressing?' Part of me wants to agree with her, but I don't know that it's that simple. There does seem to be something essentially unsecular about poetry: both in traditional, oral cultures and in our own, people rely on poetry to convey truths about matters of life and death that are accessible in no other way. In contemporary America, poetry offers many people—including poets—the consolation they no longer find in traditional religion."*

* Kathleen Norris, "Symposium on Writing and Spirituality," *Manoa: A Pacific Journal of International Writing*, 1995, p. 116.

THEOLOGY, POETRY

What is deepest and most deeply felt in life, the transitoriness of human beings, illness, death, the vanity of opinions and convictions, cannot be expressed in the language of theology, which for centuries has responded by turning out perfectly rounded balls, easy to roll but impenetrable. Twentieth-century poetry, or what is most essential in it, gathers data on the ultimate in the human condition and elaborates, to handle the data, a language which may or may not be used by theology.

DISCREET CHARM OF NIHILISM

First

First, a fringe of the aristocracy cultivating literature and art, elegant, freed from the coarser superstitions. And churches filled with the pious, the scent of their incense and their prayers. They would come to a common frame of mind. It would take a hundred and fifty years.

Opium for the People

Religion, opium for the people. To those suffering pain, humiliation, illness, and serfdom, it promised a reward in an afterlife. And now we are witnessing a transformation. A true opium for the people is a belief in nothingness after death—the huge solace of thinking that for our betrayals, greed, cowardice, murders we are not going to be judged.

Religion and Politics

It is understandable that there are those who prefer nothing to religion, especially religion with nationalistic baggage (Bosnia, Northern Ireland). There is ample experience to show that men envelop themselves in sublime goals, purity, and the nobility of a highfalutin spiritual domain, in order to pretend they don't know what their hands are doing.

Religions

All great religions—Christianity, Buddhism, Judaism, Islam—have a vision of man as judged after death, with a visible predilection for the image of a contention between the Accuser and the Defender. Sometimes there is a scale to weigh sins and good deeds. In Tibetan Buddhism the judge is the Master of Death and in coming to his verdict he is assisted by pebbles, black ones cast on a balance by the Accuser, white ones cast by the Defender. All religions recognize that our deeds are imperishable; in Buddhism this is called karma.

After It Had Been Fulfilled

A prophet, as he called himself, of European nihilism, Nietzsche used to say with pride "we, nihilists" and defined what would be the "most blatant form of nihilism." It would be "a view according to which any belief, any conviction would be by necessity false, simply because *there is no true world*." He called this "a godlike way of thinking." For his master and teacher Schopenhauer, he had an epithet: "decadent."

He would probably not be very happy with the use made of his oeuvre during the hundred years since his death. After all, what he valued was courage. And today courage is required to dissent from his views.

Poor Schopenhauer

Why should he be the philosopher whose name appears anytime a pedigree needs to be produced for European nihilism? He doesn't deserve it. If for no other reason, for the place his philosophy assigned to saintliness and art.

To the extent that he was influenced by Asian religion, liberation meant for him throwing off the burden of karma. Only in coffeehouse folklore is Nirvana identified with nothingness. According to Schopenhauer, Nirvana could not be expressed in the language of Samsara, of the illusory world: it implied just the opposite.

Vertical Axis

Up and down. One may wonder at the image of Ascension in the New Testament, but the vertical axis rules everywhere in the noncorporeal world. Thus the subterranean Hades of the Greeks and Sheol of the Jews. In Dante, Hell is below, Purgatory somehow higher, Paradise above; in the Tibetan Book of the Dead, Bardo, the intermediary state after death, allows for a movement up to better incarnations, or down to inferior incarnations.

Prediction

Vladimir Solovev in his work *Three Conversations*, 1900, tells about a sect of hole worshippers in Russia. They would bore a hole in the wall of a hut and would pray to it: "O holy hole!"

A Quotation

From "Lot's Escape" by Aleksander Wat

"Balzac, Stendhal, generations of novelists who uncovered the piteous backstage of human motives and actions, who ferreted out every proof of the degradation of human nature, down to the very bottom of man's dreams"—meditated Lot, and grew scared. He was endowed with an innate admiration for everything well executed, well written, of a proper caliber—and he felt even greater fear when he realized that no one was, any longer, concerned with "what," only with "how," that we have become indifferent to content and react, not even to form, but to technique, to technical efficiency itself.

A FLAW

Poetry, every art, is a flaw and reminds human societies that we are not healthy, even if we confess it with difficulty.

The complex of Tonio Kröger in Thomas Mann: an artist, aware of his affliction, envies average people. Early, I discovered this in my own way.

CHILDISHNESS

A poet as a child among the adults. He is aware of his childishness and must incessantly pretend he participates in the actions and mores of the adults.

A flaw: awareness of being a child inside; i.e., a naïvely emotional creature constantly endangered by the coarse laughter of the grownup.

DISLIKE

My dislike of discussing poetic form and aesthetic theories; i.e., of everything that encloses us in one role. It came from my feeling of shame; I did not want quietly to accept the verdict sentencing me to be a poet.

I envied J.P. How was it that he felt at ease in the skin of a poet? Did that mean he did not feel in himself a flaw, a dark tangle, the fear of the defenseless, or did he decide that nothing of all that should transpire outside?

ALEXANDRIA

In my early youth I got somewhere a conviction that "alex-
andrianism" meant a weakening of creative impulse and a pro-
liferation of commentaries on great works of the past. Today I
do not know whether this is true, yet I have lived to the epoch
when a word does not refer to a thing, for instance a tree, but
to a text on a tree, which text was begotten by a text on a tree,
and so on. "Alexandrianism" meant "decadence." Then for a
long time concerns about this game were abandoned, but what
about an epoch which is unable to forget anything?

Museums, libraries, photographs, reproductions, film archives.
And amid that abundance individuals who do not realize that
around them an omnipresent memory hovers and besieges, at-
tacks their tiny consciousness.

IN A LANDSCAPE

In a landscape that is nearly totally urban, just by the freeway, a pond, rushes, a wild duck, small trees. Those who pass on the road feel at that sight a kind of relief, though they would not be able to name it.

SOMEBODY DIFFERENT

I and them. To what extent can they be reached? A poet knows that he is taken by them for somebody different from what he is, and that's how it will be after his death, no sign from the other world arriving to correct the mistake.

THE PAST

The past is *inaccurate*. Whoever lives long enough knows how much what he had seen with his own eyes becomes overgrown with rumor, legend, a magnifying or belittling hearsay. "It was not like that at all!"——he would like to exclaim, but will not, for they would have seen only his moving lips without hearing his voice.

UNMANLY

Writing poetry is considered an unmanly occupation. Practicing music and painting is not so burdened. As if poetry were taking on itself the blemish accompanying all the arts, which are covertly branded effeminate.

In a tribe busy with serious occupations—i.e., war and getting food—a poet secured a place for himself as a witch-doctor, shaman, a possessor of incantations which protect, cure, or harm.

POETRY'S SEX

Poetry's sex is feminine. Is not the Muse a female? Poetry opens up and waits for a doer, a spirit, a daimon.

Probably Jeanne was right when she said she had not known anybody else as *instrumental* as I was; that is, passively submitting myself to voices, like an instrument. I took upon myself all the shames of a child among the adults, of a sick person among the healthy, of a transvestite in a woman's dress among the males. I was attacked for a lack of manly will, indefinite identity. Then I discovered in them, presumably manly and healthy, what I had been suspecting: a neurosis repressed for such a long time that it was vented in insanity.

POWER OF SPEECH

"What is not said, tends to nonexistence." It's astonishing to think about the multitude of events in the twentieth century and about the people taking part in them, and to realize that every one of those situations deserved an epic, a tragedy, or a lyric poem. But nothing—they sank, leaving only a faint trace. One can say that even the most powerful, full-blooded, active personality is hardly a shadow compared to a few well-chosen words, even if they describe no more than the rising moon.

DRESSES

Black capes, ties lavaliere, large-brimmed hats—the uniform of the bohemians. Or jeans, beards, pigtails, black sweaters. Those who by such dress want to prove that they are poets, musicians, painters. And the dislike of that uniform among the solitary who are sure enough of their work's value to manage without that paraphernalia. Yet, had they not hidden their profession under the disguise of normal people, they would have been more honest: here we demonstrate in public our shameful stigma of deviants and madmen.

SALVATION AND DAMNATION

How many among us will be saved, how many damned? Our biographies indicate the numerical preponderance of the damned. Already an excessive penchant for alcohol and other drugs indicates a weak character which escapes from confrontation with rough reality into states of intoxication. Perhaps there exist "poetic" tribes distinguished from others by such an escape from reality. Nevertheless, our clan is sufficiently international not to search for ethnic explanations.

PURSUING A GOAL

In order to accomplish something, one must dedicate oneself
to it totally, so much that our fellow men cannot even imagine
such an exclusivity. And that does not mean at all the amount
of time consumed. There are also the innumerable emotional
subterfuges practiced toward oneself, slow transformations of
personality, as if one supreme goal, beyond one's will and
knowledge, pulled in a single direction and organized destiny.

A PACT

Here is an oeuvre accomplished. If only they knew at what a price. Would not they turn away in horror? But he, the doer, had once in the past only a dim foreboding that he was signing a devilish pact. In reality there was no moment when a pen, dipped in blood from a cut finger, hesitated before putting down a signature, when it was still possible to say no.

TROPICS

A parrot screeches. Ventilators turn. An iguana walks vertically up a palm trunk, a shining ocean wave puts foam on a beach. When I was young, I was driven to despair during vacations by the boredom of obvious things. In my old age, finding myself in the tropics, I already knew that I had always searched for medicine against this horror, which lasts because it means nothing. To give a meaning, any, only to get out of this bovine, perfectly indifferent, inert reality, without aims, strivings, affirmation, negation, like an incarnated nothingness. Religions! Ideologies! Desires! Hatreds! Come to cover with your multi-colored fabric this blind thing, deprived even of a name.

PELICANS

I marvel at the incessant labor of pelicans.
Their low flights over the surface of the sea,
Poising in one place, suddenly diving
For a singled-out fish, the white splash—
All day, from six in the morning. What are views
For them, what is blue ocean, a palm tree, the horizon
(Where, at the ebb, like distant ships,
Rocks crop out and blaze,
Yellow, red, and purple)?
Don't come too close to the truth. Live with a representation
Of invisible beings who dwell above the sun,
Free, indifferent to necessity and hunger.

A BALL

He gives to the chief the head of an enemy
Whom he pounced on in the bushes by a stream
And hefted with his spear. —A scout
From the enemy village. It's a pity
It wasn't possible to capture him alive.
Then he would have been put on the sacrificial altar
And the whole village would have had a feast:
The spectacle of his being killed slowly.
They were rather tiny brown people
Presumably no more than a meter-fifty tall.
What remains of them are some ceramics,
Though they did not know the potter's wheel.
Something else, too: found in the tropical jungle
A granite ball, immense, incomprehensible.
How, without knowing iron, could they dress the granite,
Give it a perfectly spheric shape?
They worked it for how many generations?
What did it mean to them? The opposite
Of everything that passes and perishes? Of muscles, skin?
Of leaves crackling in a fire? A lofty abstraction
Stronger than anything because it is not alive?

THOSE FANTASIES

Those fantasies, those pageants constructed by the human mind above the horror of life. All arts, all myths and philosophies: yet they are not limited to staying in their own lofty zone. For from them, from dreams of the mind, this planet arises, such as we know it, transformed and being transformed by mathematical equations.

INSERTING A MEANING

Inserting a meaning occurs constantly, for works of art (of poetry, of painting, of music) enrich the register of existing things, while every existing thing calls for something, and it is not enough to say simply: it *is*. Inserting a meaning into a pine or a mountain is very difficult, it is a little easier in the case of the creations of man, that being who incessantly strives, expects, desires. Hence the repeated attempts to name the strivings hidden in an oeuvre.

Yet past events also call for a meaning, as it is difficult to stop at one word, simply saying they were. Was not Marxism just an act of inserting a meaning into the history of the nineteenth century?

And inserting a meaning into one's own life. Something must correspond to something, something must result from something. Perhaps so that things just plain stupid and dishonest find an explanation.

LEANING INTO

Daily occurrences lean every day into history. Both a human being and a thing turn one side to what is now, while with the other they look toward us or our successors out of the depth of past time.

Scraps of paper, telephones, meetings—i.e., daily routines—quickly become merely ridiculous, but later on grow to a monumental size, as they are parts of a totality carved out of the whole of experience in which many details irrevocably perish.

People, dependent as they are upon little things, are undefined and elude their own grasp or the grasp of others, yet with time they, together with little things, acquire traits that can be described, characters, like the surface of the earth, which only from a distance shows the folds of its mountain chains and the nervous system of its rivers.

A WARNING

Little animals from cartoons, talking rabbits, doggies, squirrels, as well as ladybugs, bees, grasshoppers. They have as much in common with real animals as our notions of the world have with the real world. Think of this, and tremble.

HOW IT WILL BE

Intuitions of an artist. He sees in a sudden flash, lasting a second, his oeuvre as it works in unforseeable structures after two or three hundred years.

His oeuvre in two or three hundred years. If the language in which it was written exists. And thus a dependence, how great, upon a multitude of fools who, using that language, will pull it down, and upon the wise who will lift it up. How many of the first, how many of the second?

Envies of the artists. Though comic, it is not a joyful spectacle. Each one hates every other like poison. Observing this for years, you have dark thoughts, for it's like a paradigm of our human condition. The only difference is that in the struggle for life, money, love, security, the object of struggle consists in worldly goods, tangible here and now, while the fame of a poem or of a canvas is totally abstract. The person will die and will have no use for that fame. Yet what is at stake is an image of oneself. Flattering opinions about an achievement are a beautifying mirror, unfavorable, a distorting mirror, where even traits not so bad by nature appear monstrous.

Transfer that to relations between men and women: chases, fulfillments, dramas, and always the same thing involved—an image of oneself, of one's beauty, attractiveness, male vigor, etc.

WARMTH

Every moment in that community of artists, writers, and scholars was a densely woven fabric of conflicts, friendships, aggressive-defensive alliances, and, above all, of gossip about everybody's private life. So absorbing was their submersion in the moment that its peculiar nature escaped their attention. Only the flow of time revealed it, and then one might wonder. One day, suddenly, faces perfectly familiar bore their mark of passed years, wrinkled, bleak, with gray hair or a shining baldness. This sad sight was accompanied by a shock of realization: of course, intensity is maintained by the bodily presence and animal warmth of those who are persons and organisms at the same time. When vital energy weakens, and, together with it, its radiation, the cold of the approaching glacier is felt. The big wall advances irresistibly, crushing little rabbits, froggies, teeny people and their games. Later on, there is only the history of arts, letters, and sciences. Nothing of what transpired can be faithfully reproduced, and doctoral dissertations try to dig up details in vain. A few names survive, and a question doomed to remain unanswered: Where did it all go?

THAT

It looks as if *that*, ready, formed in every detail, waited nearby, at a hand's stretching, and had I caught it, I would not have drawn the thing out of the nothingness all around, but taken, as if from a shelf, an object already existing.

A DISCOVERY

They could not understand how that poet could write poems cynical and patriotic, praising the rulers and deriding the rulers. Why he seemed to be a believer, then a skeptic; joyful, then a total pessimist. This occurred, however, when the individual was considered a kind of castle or fortress from which one would make sallies into the world.

Then people discovered civilization as a multitude of interlacing voices, as an orchestra in which every man is by turns one or another instrument. That weakening of substance, that doubting of any essence, deplorable and even called "the death of man," opened to us the new dimension of an incessantly renewable *theatrum*.

FUTURE

Premises for a society of the future. Innumerable varieties of mental illness, the insane walking in the streets and talking to themselves, as today in California, a widespread licence in sex, drugs, and crime. Thence a need to gather in small communities united by their respect for reason, common sense, and purity of habit. Perhaps even poetry survives amid the generalized savagery, now health in the midst of sickness, just as once it was sickness in the midst of health.

LABYRINTH

He happened to live at a time when man began to adore the labyrinth of his mind. That was precisely the meaning of the frenetic activity of poets and artists. A combination of words or colors on a canvas replaced questions addressed to the sky, the earth, the sea, to stars and clouds, from which no answer was expected anymore. He should have been glad, for he was a setter of words. Yet something in him resisted, and he tried to comprehend where his lack of assent came from. —Oh yes, he said, I was a child from provinces where in a little wooden church people prayed to a Deity with a human body, and the sun and the moon, carved in linden wood, made up his retinue. Thoroughly old-fashioned, I composed hymns and odes, making use of my mind just as I used paper and my pen, not caring to pay it special honors.

A COUNTRY OF DREAMS

The country of dreams has its own geography. Any time I enter it, I recognize the same vectors of direction, bearings of roads in the mountains, the way you have to turn in order to come upon the proper street. Not a repetition of the same details, for they change, but as it were an encoded spatial memory, yet taken from where, from what landscapes once seen, it is difficult to tell.

HOLLYWOOD

Let us imagine a poet gets in his hands the Hollywood crowd, those financiers, directors, actors and actresses. And that he is fully aware of the crime perpetrated every day on millions of human beings by money, which acts not in the name of any ideology but exclusively for the purpose of multiplying itself. What penalty would be adequate? He hesitates between slitting their bellies and disemboweling them; locking them together behind barbed wire in the hope that they would start to eat each other, beginning with the fattest potentates; grilling them on a small fire; throwing them, bound, onto an anthill. However, as he interrogates them and sees them humble, trembling, obsequious, fawning, not at all remembering their own arrogance, he is discouraged. Their guilt is as elusive as that of the party bureaucrats in an authoritarian state. The closest thing to justice might be to kill the whole lot. He shrugs, and sets them free.

MILDER

With age his fierceness abated and there swelled in him, along with tolerance, an all-embracing doubt. He would sit in the dark before the stage of a puppet show and watch the chases, prayers, swaggers, repentances, recognizing in them his own nonsense.

A POLISH POET

It is only through great effort that a Polish poet overcomes in himself a heritage preserved through language—that of concern about the fate of a country squeezed between two world powers. In this he differs from a poet writing in a happier tongue.

A Kurdish poet is concerned exclusively with the fate of the Kurds. For an American poet, the notion of an "American fate" does not exist. A Polish poet is always in between.

From that clash of two forces pulling in opposing directions, the specific character of Polish poetry should emerge—visible in poems having nothing to do with history, such as the erotic poetry of Anna Swir.

A complete liberation from the gravitational force of the local and provincial condemns a poet to imitate foreign models.

A poet, thrown into the international bouillabaisse where, if anything can be distinguished at all, it is only lumps of overboiled fish and shrimp, suddenly discovers that he sits firmly in his province, his town, his countryside, and begins to bless it.

DISTILLATION

Sorrow, grief, self-reproach, regret, shame, anxiety, desperation—and thus every day—and the poetry spun out of all this is clear, solid, concise, nearly classical. Who can understand it?

If only not to hide. For whoever pretends he does not have that other, dark side exposes himself to the vengeance of the spinners of Fate.

LEARNING

To believe you are magnificent. And gradually to discover that
you are not magnificent. Enough labor for one human life.

IS IT SO?

Nothing better can happen than to bid farewell to one's past life, taken as no more than a commentary to a couple of poems.

A GOAL

On one side there is luminosity, trust, faith, the beauty of the earth; on the other side, darkness, doubt, unbelief, the cruelty of the earth, the capacity of people to do evil. When I write, the first side is true; when I do not write, the second is. Thus I have to write, to save myself from disintegration. Not much philosophy in this statement, but at least it has been verified by experience.

THE NOVEL

A novel should interest, thrill, and move us. If it does not, it lacks the traits of a true novel. By nature sentimental and melodramatic, it resembles a fairy tale. This has often been forgotten from the moment the novel was charged with a multitude of duties.

MELODRAMA

Melodrama: The parents marry her, not to the man she loved. Married, she becomes in secret the mistress of her ex-fiancé, now a friend of the family (and a wealthy man), who dies and leaves her his estate. She rejects her parents and slaps her mother in the face when the mother visits her. The mother puts a curse on her daughter. And a mother's curse should fulfill itself. One of the plots in one novel, Selma Lagerlöf's *Gösta Berling*.

A FAIRY TALE

The novel as a fairy tale: the voice of the teller should be heard in it. He is present with his measures of good and evil, but he should not tell about himself. Had he been telling about himself he would prove he lacked maturity and peace of mind, traits necessary in a fairy-tale narrator. One more feature of the novel: magnanimity.

A DESIRE

A desire to open oneself before people and to tell everything about one's life. Impossible. Unless one writes a psychological novel, which, besides, would be very far from the truth. It would consist in a self-accusing confession, and we know a scrupulous conscience accuses its bearer of smaller transgressions in order to hide bigger ones.

GUILT

The longer one's life, the more torments of memory. Only a part is remembered, and that's already a blessing. Yet even that is enough to disturb a peace so highly desired. To confess, to unload one's guilt? But memory preserves on the same level moments of humiliation in school, social blunders, tactless behavior, horrible defeats, sins. In other words, everything that belies our image of ourselves as brave, heroic, pure, good-hearted. To whom would one confess these things: "I made a fool of myself, you should have seen their glances!" Or: "I knew that they, though they would not say it, thought I behaved poorly." Or: "They bet on me and I lost." Or: "At a moment that was decisive for me, I failed." Where is contrition, which the catechism divides into perfect or not perfect, if it is impossible to distinguish between improper behavior at the table and wounding or killing a human being?

MONOLOGUES

Kenneth Rexroth, listening to our conversations, said: "You don't know how to talk to each other, you just exchange monologues." He hit upon a trait of Central Europeans (not only Poles?). But we are aware of it and it makes us uneasy, for the personal line and the tribal line intersect here. Me? Or the civilization in which I was raised?

IN AFRICA

"So, here you are in Africa. Are you happy?" they asked a black poet from America. "None of those abominable whites, only black people." "The trouble is that I despise the stupidity and ignorance of the blacks. I solace myself by thinking that I come from an exceptionally intelligent African tribe."

LONGINGS

Longings, great loves, faith, hope—and all that derived from self-persuasion: thinking thus, he recognized in what the nineteenth century was different from his own. The other was a century of emotions, affections, and melodrama—and perhaps to be envied for its force of feeling.

TO WASH

At the end of his life, a poet thinks: I have plunged into so many of the obsessions and stupid ideas of my epoch! It would be necessary to put me in a bathtub and scrub me till all that dirt was washed away. And yet only because of that dirt could I be a poet of the twentieth century, and perhaps the Good Lord wanted it, so that I was of use to Him.

MY IDEAL

My ideal of virtue: those who served the cause of the mind and preserved that passion beyond eighty and to the end.

DATES

He was born, let us say, in 1811. And, still alive in 1896, should he have been concerned with what would happen to mankind, his country, his city in the twentieth century? Completely integrated into the manners and worries of his little circle, he would have been busy enough with making assessments of his contemporaries, their views, accomplishments, their associations, etc. Yet already the horrors of the twentieth century were in preparation, which he was not to see. Dante, conversing with the damned in Hell, knew what had happened after the death of those wretches and they would not have been surprised hearing that from him. But what could a new Dante writing, say, in 1960, and burdened therefore with the knowledge of his era, have told to the souls of the nineteenth century?

I SAW

I was there, and I know, because I have seen. I am surrounded by people who were born later, yet they believe that they must know, at least something, of those things. In fact, they know nothing, one detail or two, at best. It is the same with the particulars of my biography and the books I have written. We imagine we are observed and are of concern to someone. They have heard something, if only vaguely; one of my books fell into their hands and upon it they form a judgment of the others.

IF ONLY

If only we could believe that everything ends with death. Then there would be no fear that our past deeds may be shown to us, to the accompaniment of enormous laughter. Nor would we be faced with our own province of the world, to which we had been attached, and forced to watch with clear awareness the stupidity and evil of the living. We would have to remember the worry of Mickiewicz, who used to say it is hard for a spirit to act without a body.

DECENCY

When I was, as they say, in harmony with God and the world, I felt I was false, as if pretending to be somebody else. I recovered my identity when I found myself again in the skin of a sinner and nonbeliever. This repeated itself in my life several times. For, undoubtedly, I liked the image of myself as a decent man, but, immediately after I put that mask on, my conscience whispered that I was deceiving others and myself.

The notion of *sacrum* is necessary but impossible without experiencing sin. I am dirty, I am a sinner, I am unworthy, and not even because of my behavior but because of evil sitting in me. And only when I conceded that it was not for me to reach so high have I felt that I was genuine.

IT APPEARS

It appears that my oeuvre is Christian and even (practically) irreproachable according to the criteria of Catholic theology. I am not so sure, though I like to hear this. Certainly, it stands out against the background of twentieth-century poetry, also Polish poetry, which is agnostic or atheist. Yet the religious content of my poems is not the result of design by a believer; it grew out of my doubts, turmoil, and despair, as they searched for a form. If not for a strong heretical seasoning, the religious content would not have been there. Thus, my resistance to being squeezed into the rubric of "Catholic poet" was well founded.

This jubilee of mine, these flowers, the applause, and the toasts. If only they knew what I thought. It was like a cold weighing on a balance of my gains and my losses. Losses are false words that have issued from my pen, already irrevocable because they have been printed and will remain forever, and precisely these will be the most alluring for people and repeated most often. I asked myself whether it must be so that one can write a few truly good things only by paying with the deformation of one's life, as in my case, and also with trash on the way to a few notes perfectly pure.

THE LANGUAGE

The desire for truth is confronted with poems, with tales written by you long ago. And then you are ashamed, because it was all sheer myth. Neither did any of it happen, nor did you feel the feelings contained therein. The language itself unfurled its velvet yarn in order to cover what, without it, would equal nothing.

PROFIT

So shy he suffered tortures in society, unmannered, without the
elementary rules of *Kinderstube*, sweating, blushing—and the
same he as an actor in the *theatrum* of black tie, women's
evening gowns, parties, and banquets. Such a role should have
been assigned to somebody better prepared. Yet precisely from
that lack of preparation came his ability to grasp everything
that, under the surface of form, is uncouth, awkward, exagger-
ated, ludicrous, oversensitive, improper, foolish—like a run in
a stocking, the lost heel of a slipper, the lack of a tampon
urgently needed. Women seem to be closer to the everyday
disorder of viscous reality—though they are brave. Just now,
behind the "Ladies" door, they snap their bags and powder
their noses. It seems they fit better the metaphor of our exis-
tence, which consists in continuous pretending that everything
is all right and in hiding a basic incongruity.

FALLING IN LOVE

Tomber amoureux. To fall in love. Does it occur suddenly or gradually? If gradually, when is the moment "already"? I would fall in love with a monkey made of rags. With a plywood squirrel. With a botanical atlas. With an oriole. With a ferret. With a marten in a picture. With the forest one sees to the right when riding in a cart to Jaszuny. With a poem by a little-known poet. With human beings whose names still move me. And always the object of love was enveloped in erotic fantasy or was submitted, as in Stendhal, to a "cristallisation," so it is frightful to think of that object as it was, naked among the naked things, and of the fairy tales about it one invents. Yes, I was often in love with something or someone. Yet falling in love is not the same as being able to love. That is something different.

BUT

Why, yes, this current really ran through me, and really, I, shrunken, hunched, continue to be the same instrument. How is this possible?

CONTRAST

Incredulity as to the doer comes from the contrast between weaknesses of the body and an accomplished oeuvre. "How was it possible? Did I write all this? Should we believe in the participation of some supernatural powers?"

THE COMPLAINT OF A CLASSIC

The complaint of a classic—i.e., of a poet who instead of vanguard pursuits busied himself with polishing the language of his predecessors: "I was perfectly aware of how little of the world is scooped up by the net of my clauses and phrases." Like a monk, sentencing himself to ascesis, tormented by erotic visions, I would take shelter in rhythm and the order of syntax, because I was afraid of my chaos.

WHAT A FATE

What a life, what a fate! Absolutely impossible to set it in a logical sequence of cause and effect: too many lacunae which could be filled only by miraculous accidents of divine intervention.

REVERSE TELESCOPE

Probably nothing can be accomplished without a belief in one's superiority. This is achieved by looking at the accomplishments of others as if through a reverse telescope. Later, it is difficult not to be aware of the harm done.

WATERING CAN

Of a green color, standing in a shed alongside rakes and spades, it comes alive when it is filled with water from the pond, and an abundant shower pours from its nozzle, in an act, we feel it, of charity toward plants. It is not certain, however, that the watering can would have such a place in our memory, were it not for our training in noticing things. For, after all, we have been trained. Our painters do not often imitate the Dutch, who liked to paint still lifes, and yet photography contributes to our paying attention to detail and the cinema taught us that objects, once they appear on the screen, would participate in the actions of the characters and therefore should be noticed. There are also museums where canvases glorify not only human figures and landscapes but also a multitude of objects. The watering can has thus a good chance of occupying a sizable place in our imagination, and, who knows, perhaps precisely in this, in our clinging to distinctly delineated shapes, does our hope reside, of salvation from the turbulent waters of nothingness and chaos.

A WANDERER

Weaknesses of old age yet in my dreams wanderings in the mountains without effort, as in the poem by Po Chü-i, in which he, an old man, suddenly transformed in a dream, walks effortlessly with his stick.

AGAIN

Again I was flying in my dream. As if my old body contained, prior to live beings, the possibility of all movements, flying, swimming, crawling, running.

IN THAT CITY

It was a corpse of a city. The smallest heaps of rubble had been removed, lawns and flower beds were arranged, benches placed in newly delineated squares. Only there were no people. From time to time a couple of tourists would stop by the wall and slowly decipher letters on a memorial plaque.

YOU DON'T KNOW

You have no idea what is going on in the heads of people who walk by you. Their ignorance is hard to imagine and it can be discovered only by accident. This does not mean you are wise and they are stupid: simply that everyone garners information up to a certain level only, and is unable to reach higher. Space is limited, and they may be unaware of what is happening in the next street. Also, time is limited, and events, which for you happened yesterday, for them are sunken in the fog of an indefinite past. Thus TV, print can transform and alter as they please everything that is and has been. We should wonder not at the power of propaganda but at the modest amount of knowledge which somehow gets through.

O !

O objects of my desire, for whose sake I was able to practice asceticism, to be ardent, heroic, what pity I feel any time I think of your lips and hands and breasts and bellies consigned to bitter earth!

FROM MY DENTIST'S WINDOW

Extraordinary. A house. Tall. Surrounded by air. It stands. In the middle of a blue sky.

AUTUMN

Cathedral of my enchantments, autumn wind,
I grew old giving thanks.

WHERE DOES IT COME FROM?

Where does it come from? These lips, twenty years old, lightly touched by carmine red, this chestnut hair in sprays—too loose to say locks—these beautiful eyes in a frame of lashes and brows, proclaiming what? She was born at a time when I was teaching Dostoevsky and trying to cope with the realization that I was old.

There is no end to being born, and I, if allowed to continue to live, would sink again and again, dazzled by wonder and desire.

A CASTLE FROM A DREAM

The city was castle-like, compact, dense, multilayered, like the edifices of Piranesi. Red brick predominated—it signified civilization—and, on the other side of the river, wilderness began. He marched quickly; his companions, a he and a she, could hardly keep up. And suddenly he realized how abstraction changes into reality: the spicy scents from stores, an enticing vapor from passed-by kitchens, huge flitches of hams, taverns full of wine drinkers, oh, to be thus restored to the senses, only that and nothing else.

A LITTLE TREATISE ON COLORS

The leaves of the oaks are like the leather of bookbinding. How to speak otherwise of them, when in October they take on a brown hue and are as if leathery, ready to be set with gold. Why this excessive poverty of language any time we deal with colors? What do we have at our disposal when we try to name the splendor of colors? Some leaves are yellow, some red, and is that all? But there are also yellow-red, and flame-red, and bull's blood-red (why this recourse to comparisons?). And birches. Their leaves are like small, pale-yellow coins, sparsely attached to twigs which are of what hue? Lilac, from the lilacs, and violet, from the violet (again, these unwieldy comparisons). How does the yellow of birch leaves differ from the yellow of aspens, underlaid with copper, stronger and stronger, till copper wins. A copper color? Again a thing, copper. And probably only green and yellow are deeply rooted in the language, for blue the etymologists associate with *flavus*, yellow, while red again, in its old Norse forms, goes back to trees, the rowan or *reynir*, the mountain ash, or perhaps to rust. Is the language so resistant because our eyes are not very attentive to details of nature unless they serve a practical purpose? In October, pumpkins ripen in the fields and their color is orange. Why this recourse to orange, how many eyes saw oranges in a northern country?

I put all this down, for I have encountered difficulty in describing autumn in the valley of the Connecticut River in a precise and simple manner, without the props of comparison and metaphor.

TANGLEWOOD

To dive into a tanglewood. Early, in childhood, homemade ornithological atlases and maps of imaginary countries; then, when he grew up, a pale green jungle of literary works, of names and portraits. A reader of "Literary News" and of professorial books on great romantic poets, he undertook expeditions through sentences too difficult for him and tried to understand words taken from foreign languages. And thus it was to be always, a tanglewood promising to open into something tomorrow—mystery, hope. Unfortunately, this was a time when elementary fear of death was imposed upon everyone and everyone had to move naked, like an insect taken from under bark and thrown onto a stone slab. He, however, at the first opportunity, would dive into his tanglewood, which had provided refuge for generations and was more real than any visible world.

How to explain to foreigners that he lived through years of war and terror only in appearance present but in fact residing where Nature and History have no access?

A STRATEGY

He was everywhere, on a train carrying prisoners to the gulag, in a city trembling at a doorbell at dawn, in a prison from which the sentenced to death were walked out and loaded into trucks. He hated the Empire, yet he had to hide this. He was a poet, and keeping constantly in mind that these things were going on, simultaneously and close by, would make writing poetry impossible. Besides, he was writing for those who, though theoretically aware of what was going on, did not want to absorb it with their imaginations. For these reasons, feeling he failed in his duty to give testimony, he searched for a means, when writing, to preserve, unspoken, the presence of horror between his words and lines.

THE LAW OF THE EARTH

A child weeps bitter tears reading about the destruction of the city of Milano by the emperor Frederick Barbarossa. Grown up, he does not know for sure whether such a thing really took place in history, yet the memory of those pages in a book for children is so vivid to him that it determines his decisions. Evil is equated in his mind with naked force which wins against the desires of our heart, and when he discovers that this is the law of the earth, he hates the law of the earth.

IN HER DIARY

Zofia Nalkowska writes in her diary on April 14, 1943, when the Germans were killing the remaining population of the Warsaw ghetto:

"Why do I torture myself so, why am I ashamed to live, why can't I stand it anymore? Is the world horrible? What happens is in accord with the rest of Nature, is bestial—therefore, such as the nonhuman world is, *so the world is.* Cats and birds, birds among themselves, birds and insects, men and fish, wolves and sheep, bacteria and humans. Everything is like that. Is the world horrible? The world is *ordinary*, this must be assumed. The world is like that, the world is ordinary. What is strange is only my feeling of horror, mine and that of others like myself."

Much courage is needed to recognize the mass crimes of the twentieth century as *ordinary*. Animals do not sit in their offices and do not elaborate plans and then proceed to their execution in cold blood. Yet the stronger killing the weaker is the rule, probably since the beginning of life on earth. Nalkowska is right—going against those who affirm, as does the French philosopher Levinas, that God departed in 1941 when Auschwitz was established. Her atheism frees her from a quarrel with the Creator who must be held responsible for the sufferings of human beings. Not only human beings, for he should be accused of arranging the whole structure of live matter.

An atheist should accept the world as it is. But then whence comes our protest, our scream: "No!" Precisely, this excludes us from Nature, determines our incomprehensible oddity, makes us a lonely species. Here, in a moral protest against the order of the world, in our asking ourselves where this scream of horror comes from, the defense of the peculiar place of man begins.

BEYOND MY STRENGTH

To recognize the world as *ordinary* is beyond my strength. For me it is magnificent and horrible, impossible to bear. Everything indicates that either it was created by the devil or, as it is now, is the result of a primordial catastrophe. In the second case, the death on the cross of a divine Redeemer acquires full meaning.

Our tearing away from the *ordinariness* of the world is like the efforts of a fly whose leg is stuck in glue. No logic in this unwillingess to accept. We must concede, however, that the logic offered by the Book of Genesis is no better. Our first parents sinned, were expelled from Paradise, and we continue to live in the state of fallen creatures. But what happened to those animals in the Garden of Eden? Did the sin of man change First Nature, as the cabalists maintain, into a deteriorated Second Nature, which has been longing ever since for a return to the moment when again the lion would lie down with the lamb?

WHY RELIGION?

Instead of leaving to theologians their worries, I have constantly meditated on religion. Why? Simply because *someone* had to do this. To write on literature or art was considered an honorable occupation, whereas any time notions taken from the language of religion appeared, the one who brought them up was immediately treated as lacking in tact, as if a silent pact had been broken.

Yet I lived at a time when a huge change in the contents of the human imagination was occurring. In my lifetime Heaven and Hell disappeared, the belief in life after death was considerably weakened, the borderline between man and animals, once so clear, ceased to be obvious under the impact of the theory of evolution, the notion of absolute truth lost its supreme position, history directed by Providence started to look like a field of battle between blind forces. After two thousand years in which a huge edifice of creeds and dogmas has been erected, from Origen and Saint Augustine to Thomas Aquinas and Cardinal Newman, when every work of the human mind and of human hands was created within a system of reference, the age of homelessness has dawned. How could I not think of this? And is it not surprising that my preoccupation was a rare case?

PITY

In the ninth decade of my life, the feeling which rises in me is pity, useless. A multitude, an immense number of faces, shapes, fates of particular beings, and a sort of merging with them from inside, but at the same time my awareness that I will not find anymore the means to offer a home in my poems to these guests of mine, for it is too late. I think also that, could I start anew, every poem of mine would have been a biography or a portrait of a particular person, or, in fact, a lament over his or her destiny.

HELENE

Here we are on the other side.

Expeditions. Demesnes were leased out. Steam rose from the cinders.

It must be Helene over there, dancing between the flames.

Perhaps she knows now the secret of particular existence.

All my life I tried in vain to comprehend it.

You suffered much, Helene, and said nothing.

Hungry, you didn't even ask for help.

And hospitals, that bodily misery wanting to love itself;

Hating itself, it weeps in a dirty hallway.

Who would have thought, Helene, that our youth would turn out this way?

The garden glowed in the sun and summer lasted forever.

Later for a long time we learn how to bear what is borne by others.

And how to bless a moment if it is without pain.

HELENE'S RELIGION

On Sunday I go to church and pray with all the others.
Who am I to think I am different?
—Enough that I don't listen to what the priests blabber in
their sermons.
Otherwise, I would have to concede that I reject common
sense.
I have tried to be a faithful daughter of my Roman Catholic
Church.
I recite the Our Father, the Credo and Hail Mary
Against my abominable unbelief.
It's not up to me to know anything about Heaven or Hell.
But in this world there is too much ugliness and horror.
So there must be, somewhere, goodness and truth.
And that means somewhere God must be.

YOKIMURA

Once I saw on TV a cemetery of unborn babies, with little graves on which Japanese women lit candles and laid flowers. I put myself for a moment in the place of one of them who was leaning over to put down a spray of chrysanthemums.

—My son, you were conceived in love, that's all I will ever know about you.

You might have heard from me about the terror of life on earth, but you were spared.

About how we are visited by misfortune and cannot understand why we, who are unique, must be struck like the others.

Perhaps you would have had a life like mine and, clenching your teeth, would have borne your fate for years, for one has to.

Suffering, I thought that perhaps you, my son, had inherited my accursed tenacity and capacity for self-delusion.

So then I felt relief, saying to myself that at least you were safe.

In nonbeing as in a cradle or a cocoon of silk down.

Who would you have been? Every day I would have trembled to know what was winning in you: a portent of greatness or of defeat—one tiny grain is enough to tip the balance.

Either people's gratitude and respect or an embittered man's four walls.

No, I am certain you would have been powerful and brave, as all those are who are begotten by love.

I made a decision and I know that was how it had to be, and I did not blame anyone.

When I bite a peach, when I look at the rising moon, when I rejoice at the sight of young cedar groves on the mountains, I taste everything in your stead, in your name.

AMERICA

A tawny and lead-gray current of swift river,
To which a man and a woman come, leading a yoke of oxen,
To found a city and to plant in the middle of it a tree.
Under this tree I used to sit at midday
And look at the low bank on the other side:
There, a marsh, rushes, a pond overgrown with duckweed
Shone as before, when the two, of unknown name, were
      alive.
I did not expect it would fall to me: the river, the city,
Here, nowhere else, the bench and the tree.

Subjects to Let

The simplest answer is that I am old and will not be able to make use of them myself. To this simple explanation, something may be added. The earth seems to me a very interesting place to stay and it's a pity one has to leave it, yet nothing can be done about it. Should I enumerate the infirmities which afflict an organism as it gets old, changing my writing into a diary of the progress of decay? Neither I nor anyone else would profit from it. Yet I must write. Since my early youth I felt the presence of a diamonion, or, if you prefer, a Muse, and if not for that companion, I would have perished. Writing, though, constantly undergoes transformations, following the transformations of our consciousness. My consciousness now is different from what it was ten or twenty and, of course, fifty years ago. It would be more correct to say: my ignorance. For many years my internal trouble could be reduced to the question: How to bear memory? I am inclined to see myself as an exception, in view of some traumatic experiences, and yet I realize all those who write are busy with remembering, whatever their age, gender, or the type of their traumas. As for myself, I believe such dwelling on oneself is harmful. This at least is an advantage of having passed eighty: the spectacle of the world, horrible as it is, appears also as highly comic and thus excessive seriousness is not indicated. At first, we try to attain as high a degree of consciousness as possible, then indulgently we welcome ignorance. At the same time, the very spectacle gains importance simply because it was performed before we existed and it's going to be performed when we are no more. It is a good thing to increase the interest of human beings in that Theatrum Mundi; a bad thing to try to persuade them that as soon as we die, it all disintegrates into nothingness. My subjects may be useful to people who are tired by literatures of confessions, by an overflowing stream of perceptions, by shapelessness of a tale about oneself. Blessed be classicism and let us hope it did not pass away forever.

A BANNER

Percy, the Prince of Northumberland's son (his elder brother, called Hotspur, appears in Shakespeare's royal chronicles), was a knight without stain or reproach. Animated with an ardor to carry the Christian faith to the heathen, he joined the Teutonic Order fighting at the frontiers of Christendom. We would have known nothing of his presence in our regions if not for an item noted down under the year 1393 in the chronicle of Lindenblat and Vigand. The Order's troops, after they crossed the river Niemen at Alytus (Aliten), marched toward Lida. The banner of Saint George was carried by Brother Rupprecht Sekendorf. This angered Percy, who considered that this honor should belong to the knights from England. He drew his sword and an armed clash was imminent, but at the last moment the elders of the Order succeeded in reconciling the parties.

Nearly six hundred years later, we learned from the list of recognized saints that the patron of knighthood, Saint George fighting a dragon, never existed.

RIVER BASINS

Remote corners of Europe. I try to imagine those provinces in the year 1811 when guests feasted and gathered mushrooms in Soplicowo, a country estate in the rural idyll "Pan Tadeusz." Something of the last phase of that world remains in my memory, the rest I reconstruct from various data. That region was the basin of the river Niemen, where only remnants of the original wilderness survived, and barges transported to Königsberg mostly agricultural products. But a little farther to the north, where the rivers were tributaries of the Dvina, the cutting of the primeval forests was still in full swing and timber was floated to Riga to enrich the German merchants there. Armed incursions into a part of a forest destined to be cut were common, as property lines were but approximately marked ("from a curved pine and a rock, turn to the right"). Riflemen, beaver trappers, beaters, also "braves"—the strong, young crews of lumber trains or of barges loaded with half-worked timber. Big money changing hands, sudden fortunes for noble families, servants accompanying their masters, prompt to use their sabers and muskets. That forest life was going on side by side with the rural life, but no description of it exists.

THE EDGE OF THE CONTINENT

It is a savage landscape of mountain slopes, steeply descending to the Pacific, canyons, coves with redwood forests, narrow creeks carved into precipitous shores. The herds of sea lions rest, swaying with a wave, or stretch on rock islets. Here, in this desolation, it is hard not to think what came before; in any case, we are prompted by a habit of imagination that looks everywhere for remnants of castles, of cities, of lost civilizations. Yet here there is nothing and even if it sounds too bold, there has never been anything except this space, the ocean, the same sunrises and sunsets. If Indians passed by or lived here, no building, not even the most primitive, not a stone, testifies to their existence. With one exception, so curious that it prompted Robinson Jeffers to write a poem about it.

Hands

Inside a cave in a narrow canyon near Tassajara
The vault of rock is painted with hands,
A multitude of hands in the twilight, a cloud of men's palms,
  no more,
No other picture. There's no one to say
Whether the brown shy quiet people who are dead intended
Religion or magic, or made their tracings

In the idleness of art; but over the division of years these
   careful
Signs-manual are now like a sealed message
Saying: "Look: we also were human; we had hands, not paws.
    All hail
You people with the cleverer hands, our supplanters
In the beautiful country; enjoy her a season, her beauty and
   come down
And be supplanted; for you also are human."

When did they leave those imprints? A thousand years earlier, a thousand years later, is of no importance. And only here, remembering dates of coronations, of battles, of the building of cathedrals, of the founding of universities, of works of painting and literature, do we realize how much content can be loaded onto the words "a thousand years," in this place, so empty. But, after all, something had to penetrate here from outside, if only because the sea is movement. For instance, the sea might one day throw up a castaway from a Japanese ship. Who was he? A simple fisherman, or, since the variety of human fates is unlimited, a samurai, a merchant, or even a poet? Torn from his ritual civilization, from his Shinto religion whose gods remained far away, he would experience loneliness so radical that it could destroy his very will to survive. And if he lived and met a tribe of local brown-skinned inhabitants, how did it occur? And what happened next? He never returned to his Japan, he did not transfer to anybody the news of his adventure, and there is no trace of him in the chronicles of mankind.

FLEAS

It was at the time when missions fell into ruin and their possessions were divided by the Mexican authorities among neighboring estates, before the appearance of Americans. The causes of the missions' downfall were multiple. The Sonoma mission disintegrated because of grizzly bears. These made a discovery, that the mission's cattle could serve as a larder of fresh meat, and ignored the Indians who guarded the herds. The mission therefore invited from the Presidio in San Francisco a few soldiers with muskets. Syphilis brought by them developed into an epidemic lethal to the Indian converts.

The golden era of huge landed estates was short but magnificent. Their growth was unrestricted and was expressed by hundreds of thousands of acres. No agriculture was practiced, only the raising of large herds of cattle and horses. The wealth derived from it expressed in sumptuous harnesses and carriages, saddles inlaid with silver, the elegant dress of cavaliers and ladies, as well as in a lively social life. One would visit neighbors, attend dancing soirees and balls, observing the forms of civility, honor, respect for the elderly, and politeness toward women. Strangely enough, that gallantry and hand-kissing, that jingle of spurs, and those furtive looks from behind fans did not have as a background marble or jasper. As Arthur Quinn relates in his history of Marin County, the houses of those nabobs did not show much regard for comfort and had hard-beaten dirt for their floors. That dirt and a warm climate favored the breeding of an immense quantity of fleas. I cannot imagine the whirling in dance of those *caballeros* and *senoritas* other than as their pretending they had only their upper parts, while he and she felt a terrible itching below and nearly fainted from the desire to stop the dance and scratch themselves, even to the point of bleeding.

Above and below—this leads to a thought about a human being pestered by parasites, the presence of which is usually passed over in silence in descriptions of phases and events of history, also in films about the past. Yet human thoughts, feelings, and decisions were practically always accompanied by fleas, lice, and bedbugs, as it was impossible to get rid of them except by burning cities, though that was done for other reasons. California Indians managed to solve the problem by burning their villages to the ground from time to time and moving to other places; it was easy, for their huts were made of reeds.

The civilization of politeness and of fleas, the pride of "the native sons" of California, came to its end when their rule was supplanted by money, innocently at first announcing its might when the first English-speaking adventurers appeared, mostly deserters from whalers. In the middle of the century a new era began, of capital gone wild and of houses with bathrooms.

ARCHAEOLOGY

Volodia Guguiev as a child dreamed of a career as an archaeologist. He became one, and made an important discovery digging in a mound close to his home, in a suburb of his city of Rostov. It proved to be the tomb of a Sarmatian princess from the second century B.C.: a little skeleton in a golden crown and a necklace studded with turquoise. What is hidden under the cities we walk—for instance, under the city of Kraków? Presumably there was a Celtic settlement once, but that was like yesterday. A long time before the appearance of Indo-Europeans, the old Europe flourished, the one of which the last trace remained in the pre-Greek island of Crete. The idea of progress contributes to our regarding people from the remote past as "primitive." If it were not for our lack of imagination, a quite different sequence might have sounded convincing: after the old myths, legends, religions, a wilderness might have taken over, inhabited by savages. Around five thousand years B.C., that is, seven thousand years ago, an agricultural civilization existed in the basin of the middle Danube, the Drava, the Vistula, and the Oder. No more than guesses, on the basis of excavations: a matriarchal civilization, little sculpted human figures, masked for some sacral purposes, a religion of the great Goddess and of other goddesses of fertility. Those people, it seems, did not associate fertility with male sperm. A woman gave birth as the earth gave birth every spring, and this virgin birth was a miracle, hence female harvest divinities. Later, in the second millennium B.C., Indo-European tribes arrived, one after the other, from the steppes of Asia, bringing their masculine gods.

And if we give them, those over whom we walk, a moment of thought? Too far in the past for their skeletons and skulls to be preserved, they are one with the soil, yet they existed, not only as an unfathomable number but also as individual beings. If our planet's destiny is to populate with souls heavens and hells, swarms of them move in unreal space, incessantly astonished by the rites, manners, and appearance of their successors, just as we would have been astonished if we'd been able to meet them.

MRS. DARWIN

Before Charles Darwin published his work *On the Origin of Species* in 1859, he had to hear many reproaches from his wife, a deeply religious person, who could not accept his decision to send to the printer so noxious a book.

—Charles—she would say—God has told us that He created man in His image and likeness. He did not say that about the ant, the bird, or the ape, or the dog or the cat. He placed man above everything alive and subjected the earth to his dominion. By what right do you deprive of his dignity a being that has the face of God and is the equal of angels?

Her husband then would answer that if he did not do it, Wallace would, since he had hit upon a similar idea.

—Charles—she replied—we should be aware of our motives. You would not have been so intent on achieving fame as a scientist, if not for your successive failures. I know you do not like to be reminded of that, but had you succeeded in becoming a physician, as you desired, you would have derived enough satisfaction from curing people, instead of trying to satisfy your ambition at any price. And had those years when you studied theology at Cambridge allowed you to become a minister of the Church, your work in a human community would have protected you from adventurism.

—You know very well where you borrowed your theory. You found it in Malthus. A bad man, Charles, cruel and indifferent to the fate of the poor. I don't believe your theory, for your observations were not made with good intent.

Charles Darwin had occasion later to think of her words, though he was at the same time quite certain that his theory of evolution was correct. So much the worse for me and for humans. The theology that can be drawn from it is nothing but that of the devil's chaplain. What good Creator would contrive such a world, an arena in which, like gladiators, individuals and whole species struggle for survival? If he watches all that, like some Roman emperor sitting in his special box, I will not pay him tribute. Happy are those who, like Emma, preserved the image of God as our Father and friend.

ONE LIFE

Against the advice of her father and uncle, who remained faithful to the principles of the Age of Reason, she would plunge into sentimental novels, swore by the poetry of Ossian, and admired Byron. She used to dance with ardor at the balls, but what she liked the most were solitary horse rides in the forests and the seclusion in which she filled pages with exalted stories in French, the language she knew better than her native Polish. Of course, she had to fall in love. Her chosen one was a handsome Russian officer, Vladimir, the governor's son. He was involved in liberal organizations but did not figure on the lists of suspects at the trial of the Decembrists.

The insistent demands of her family that she should marry were ineffectual. She pursued only Vladimir, so steadily that at last he could not resist her confession of love. Then she trembled for him when the Russo-Turkish war began and his regiment was sent to the Balkans. The news of his death at the attack on the fortress of Shumla was received by her as a sentence ending her life. Always in mourning, she chose for her only goal to find the grave of her lover and build there a mausoleum. His country was now her country and she did not want to hear of the Polish-Russian feud. She moved to Odessa, as it was closer to the Balkans and to the place where her beloved perished.

She was forty when the matter of the projected mausoleum brought her to Istanbul. There she met an emissary of the Polish émigrés in France, the novelist Michael Czajkowski, engaged in intelligence and organizational work against Russia in the Balkans. It happened that they started to live together, though Michael had a French wife in Paris and three children, and on one of his leaves added a fourth. Her dedication to the man was total. Now his country was her country; his work, her work. Money destined for the construction of the mausoleum went for the somewhat crazy purpose recommended by Michael.

Soliciting the protection of the Sultan, and justifying his act by high political considerations, Michael shifted from Roman Catholicism to Islam and adopted the name Mehmed Sadik. Now she became his official wife, though at the price of lowering her status to that of Turkish women, wearing a veil, and renouncing her cherished horse rides.

Her husband, Sadik Pasha, a politician and soldier in the Crimean War, the commander of Cossack regiments, found in Miss Sniadecka, as she was stubbornly called by the Poles, a confidante, a helper, and a bright adviser in the labyrinth of international diplomacy. She used her literary talents to write innumerable reports, memos, and political letters, so that her days and months and years were laborious.

Wild, self-willed, stubborn, indifferent to conventions and decency: so she was seen in her youth and that opinion proved to be correct. Nothing survived of her archive and we will never learn how she conquered Vladimir, what she was doing in Odessa, and in what circumstances her romance with Sadik started. Let us add that the contours of her face were sharp; eyes, black; skin, very white; and her frame, slender. The gossip that was circulated about her would fill volumes. Today, nobody would remember her existence, if not for that short time in her youth when she deigned to dance and ride together with the young Juliusz Slowacki, a future great Romantic poet. She did not pay attention to the boy's feelings, and when he revealed them, she gave him a severe sermon. And many years later, when she learned that he had written of her as the only love of his life, she shrugged.

CHUR-CHU-RAH

The system of public speech in that country seemed impenetrable to foreigners, who only wondered how people could live and even preserve a smile under so strong a pressure of obligatory phraseology. I succeeded in finding a key to that system when I remembered certain games of my childhood that we used to play in our tenement yard. Whether we were racing after each other or trading blows, we always knew that it was enough to utter the magic word and you would automatically exclude yourself from the game, becoming untouchable. That word was, I can reveal it now, Chur-chu-rah.

The monotony of speeches, papers, journalistic articles, scholarly proceedings in that country might have been unbearable, as they used a wooden language made of mandatory clichés. Against that background, the pronouncements of the few were astonishing for their brightness, color, and logic, as if made in an uncensored press. What was the secret? Those few knew a word which, when uttered, would put you out of the game, and then all prohibitions were lifted. Of course, the word was well guarded and only the initiates realized it was used. Yet a considerable number of people were familiar with it in its version that was applicable to everyday conversation, which allowed them to live and talk normally.

TRANSMISSION OF ACQUIRED TRAITS

It is not customary to write about the psychological problems of clergymen, as they seem to be a separate species, the servants of the ritual. Also that priest, let us call him Stanislaw, was of the opinion that he had no right to talk about himself, as people expected something else from him. Nevertheless, he was well aware that he lived in two zones simultaneously, one protected by silence, another which used exclusively words and notions authorized by the Catholic dogmatics.

What he carried inside could be briefly defined as dread. He even used to think that his parents transmitted to him, born after the war, their moments of terror encoded in his blood, which would mean that we inherit not only a combination of genes but also all the tremors of the organism, induced by joy and despair. A country with an exceptionally cruel history exposed everybody to dramatic situations, and the memory of atrocious events smoldered under the surface of everyday routine. Stanislaw considered that his dread of the world was the real cause of his decision to become a priest. He meditated much on the generation of his parents, coming to the conclusion that it was crippled, even sick, and, what was worse, was unwilling to realize it. If one is a slave, humiliated, slapped on the face, filled with hate but impotent, the experience marks one forever. Slave raids in Africa and the institution of slavery were re-created on the European continent, except that they were directed against white men, these slaves forced, in addition, to watch when their neighbors, also white, were killed, and forbidden to intervene under penalty of death. Stanislaw did not know and did not try to learn what his parents felt when they had to turn their eyes away from the spectacle of the annihilation of the Jews and to confess in their hearts that their desire to protect themselves was stronger than compassion or decency. Every Sunday they would go to church and somehow succeeded in patching up this contradiction. Perhaps they begged the Good Lord for forgiveness.

Father Stanislaw thought of himself as the son of people humiliated and crushed by a police state established in the name of a utopia, first of race, then of class. In the seminary, his curiosity was aroused by the history of the first centuries of the Church, when Christianity most obviously was a religion of slaves. Those who showed the slightest sign of rebellion were nailed to the crosses standing along the roads, so that their death throes testified to the invincible power of the empire.

Father Stanislaw's dread filled him with images of suffering no human protest or begging could avert. Heaven answered with silence the moans of lashed serfs, the screams of crucified slaves, and the prayers of prisoners in the twentieth-century death camps. If it was God who created this world and submitted it to the blind law of force, then He was a moral monster and it was impossible to believe in Him.

Stanislaw put his trust in God only because God delivered to torture his only Son, in other words, Himself, and whispered in His death agony with His human lips the words of utter despair. A complete lack of logic in the Christian religion was the only possible logic of faith. And yet Stanislaw did not divulge to anybody his, strange for a priest, obsession. Namely, he was unable to accept the use made of the cross. The faithful would carry around in their churches an instrument of torture as a sign of Salvation, without seeing on it a body contorted in unbearable pain, as if one could be a Christian only by renouncing empathic imagination. By turning the crucifix into abstraction, they also stripped of reality the body on the gallows or in the gas chamber, just so that they did not have to recognize that a religion of a crucified God is a religion of cosmic pain.

CARRYING A SPLINTER

Every year he would ponder what he had been spared, and that was enough to give him happiness. For when he crossed the border illegally, the same thing could have happened to him that befell a classmate of his from the Sigismundus Augustus High School, who was to spend sixteen years in the gulags. Indeed, a leading motif of his long life has been imagining the fate of his Wilno peers in the labor camps and mines of Vorkuta, though the authors of his biographies were not aware of this. He identified himself with prisoners of the polar night, and hence his ecstatic gratitude for every sunrise and every slice of bread. Yet, precisely because of this, he carried a splinter of resentment toward the so-called people of the West. He was unable to forgive not only their intellectuals, always on the lookout for a perfect tyranny, provided it was far from their homes, but also all the citizens of those countries, united by their common refusal to know.

He asked himself what to do with this splinter. The most honest thing would have been to take upon oneself the task of publicly proclaiming the truth. Unfortunately, the Empire of the Lie was powerful, and simpleminded collectors of facts could do nothing against it, since their terrifying revelations were branded as madmen's hallucinations. A more clever tactic was needed. Some bearers of the splinter would decide to serve the Empire, to take, in that manner, revenge on the villainous politicians of the West. He, however, after many hesitations, chose something else. He learned to pretend for years that he, as befits a worshipper of the intellect, was cultured, progressive, tolerant, permissive, until he became one of their luminaries, even as he bore his knowledge, which he would not reveal. And when his books gained fame and the analyses were written, no literary critic would guess that behind their philosophical meditations was the image of sufferings crying to Heaven for vengeance. Only the memory of the Vorkuta prisoners could provide an unshakable measure to distinguish good from evil, and whosoever applied it was more dangerous to the monster state than regiments and armies.

A CERTAIN POET

That poet lived all his life in a quiet provincial town, at a time when there were no wars or revolutionary upheavals. It is possible to reconstruct from his poems his circle of people. It included his father and mother, the enigmatic aunt, Adele, her husband, Victor, a young person by the name of Helene, and his close friend, the owner of a local printing shop and a philosopher, Cornelius. And those few characters were enough to bring to life a poetry of descent into the abyss and of soaring ecstasy, a testimony of dark passions, sins, and terrors.

This should lead us to conclude that the importance of an oeuvre is not measured by the importance of the events which led, one way or another, to its creation. No doubt, the facts we try to guess had no significance for the history of mankind. Whether Adele was the mistress of the poet's father, whether and why her husband tolerated that arrangement, whether the poet was jealous or simply took his mother's side, what his relationship with Helene was like, and whether it was a triangle with Cornelius as one of its sides—those components of the human cosmos are too common to have much meaning ascribed to them. And yet what depth in those stanzas where, encoded, the most ordinary human dramas glow with a glare of ultimate things, what force in the transformation of the very stuff of people's everyday life into that marvelously muscular body of verse!

That oeuvre is a warning to all those who envy poets with rich biographies, possessing at their disposal images of burning cities, of the wanderings of crazed humanity, and of murderous cohorts marching.

FATHER'S WORRIES

—Unnecessary were all those worries of yours about your washout of a son. Certainly it's painful for a solid, hardworking man to watch a lazybones who is unable to earn a penny and all his life lives at his father's expense. Yet if it were not for him, nobody today would know of the merchant from Aix. He made the name of your family famous. As to money, for the worth of his paintings you could buy all of Aix, where children used to throw stones at him.

—Easy to say today. I watched him and found in him all my weaknesses of which I was ashamed. I, too, when I was young wanted to stargaze and compose verses, but I overcame my idleness and forced myself to work. What did I get from his genius? I didn't know about it. The portrait he painted of me is not at all bad, but that was when he was still a student. Later, only daubing. Your arguments do not convince me, for a prodigal son is a heavy sorrow, and if one in thousands proves his worth, the exception changes nothing.

OEUVRE

We strove, but our goals disintegrated one after another and now we have nothing except works of art and our tribute paid to their creators.

Also sorrow and compassion. For an artist, a poet or a painter, toils and pursues every day a perfection that escapes him. He is satisfied with the result of his labor for a moment only, and is never certain whether he is good at what he does.

Many share the fate of that painter. He was not concerned with earthly possessions, he lived and dressed haphazardly, and his sacred word was: "To work." Every morning he would stand before his easel, working all day, but no sooner had he finished than he would put his canvas in the corner and forget it, to start a new picture in the morning, always with new hope. His attempt to pass the examination for the School of Beaux Arts was unsuccessful. He loved masters of painting, old and contemporary, but had no hope of equaling them. Detesting worldly life, as it would lure him away from work, he stayed apart. He lived with his model, with whom he had a son, and after seventeen years of cohabitation he married her. His paintings were systematically rejected by the Salons. He needed confirmation of his worth, but though his friends praised him, he did not believe them and considered himself a failed painter. He would kick and trample his canvases or would give them away freely. In his old age he despaired over his failure but continued to paint every day. In his native town, where he lived, he was slighted and hated; it's hard to tell why, for he did not harm anybody and helped the poor. Uncouth, in stained clothes with ripped-off buttons, he looked like a scarecrow and was a laughing-stock of children. His name was Paul Cézanne.

This tale may comfort many readers, since it confirms the familiar pattern of greatness not recognized and crowned late. However, there were numberless artists, similarly humble and hardworking, often living not far from us, whose names mean nothing today.

AMONG PEOPLE

Science and its marveling at the universe, both the macrocosm and the microcosm. But the most astonishing thing is "to be one" (Miron Bialoszewski) among the human species. To what can that species be compared? To a pulsating organism composed of autonomous tiny parts, a gigantic sea anemone, or a nebula of stars? It is impossible to think of it objectively, for horror changes into a hymn of praise, admiration into loathing. It is a species that invented good and evil, shame and guilt, ecstasy of love and passion of hatred. It reached with the creations of its mind beyond galaxies and drew its destructive power from an idea. At noon a secretary turns off her computer and goes to lunch, while all mankind preceding her turns, moves in her, like luminous lines in a glass ball. Precisely this, the refraction in her, this one being, of human millennia, of gods, demons, faiths, habits, rites, verdicts, mores, holocausts, epics—it is difficult to comprehend. She walks serenely on the earth, feeling the touch of her sweater on her small breasts, and simultaneously, deeper than consciousness, all that ever was works in her, demanding a voice. One, and there is no answer to the question whether all the past has been preserved in her genes or, on the contrary, whether, tossed onto some desert island, she would have had to start from zero. In either case, she is not just a bubble of air on a breaking wave; she exists as she, and that is probably the most enigmatic thing of all.

CHRISTOPHER ROBIN

In April of 1996 the international press carried the news of the death, at age seventy-five, of Christopher Robin Milne, immortalized in a book by his father, A. A. Milne, Winnie-the-Pooh, *as Christopher Robin.*

I must think suddenly of matters too difficult for a bear of little brain. I have never asked myself what lies beyond the place where we live, I and Rabbit, Piglet and Eeyore, with our friend Christopher Robin. That is, we continued to live here, and nothing changed, and I just ate my little something. Only Christopher Robin left for a moment.

Owl says that immediately beyond our garden Time begins, and that it is an awfully deep well. If you fall in it, you go down and down, very quickly, and no one knows what happens to you next. I was a bit worried about Christopher Robin falling in, but he came back and then I asked him about the well. "Old bear," he answered. "I was in it and I was falling and I was changing as I fell. My legs became long, I was a big person, I wore trousers down to the ground, I had a gray beard, then I grew old, hunched, and I walked with a cane, and then I died. It was probably just a dream, it was quite unreal. The only real thing was you, old bear, and our shared fun. Now I won't go anywhere, even if I'm called for an afternoon snack."

BEAUTIFUL GIRL

—Of course, I used to spend a lot of time before a mirror and I liked to look at myself. And, to be frank, I would even find in myself some whorish inclinations. Nobody is completely free of them, and in women they can be quite strong. Yet when I agreed to that session, it proved to be something else. Simply, I had no money, and to be photographed naked for a porno magazine did not seem to me to amount to much. Then I saw myself on the page in so-called natural colors, my breasts properly exposed, my hands presumably protecting a little furry animal on my mound. It was an unsettling experience. For whenever I looked at myself undressed, in a mirror, the details of the body were mine and seasoned with my myness. Also, in making love we are not, after all, a piece of meat on a dish. But here the body was completely deprived of my person. It was not unlike being in a gynecological chair, though even there we defend ourselves against total objectivization, we are not the eyes of a doctor. There is the testimony of those who return from beyond the threshold of death; they agree in one detail, even if interpretations differ according to personal beliefs. They assure us that at a certain moment one observes with indifference one's immobile mortal envelope somewhere below. What I am talking about is not unlike that experience.

PALM READING

The old eccentric liked to sit in an artists' café which also had among its customers a young, pretty, and probably happy couple. The old man was somewhat feared because of his past, which seemed taken from a legend, his looks of a sorcerer, as well as his peculiar interest in magic and chiromancy. Once the girl asked him to read their palms. Here is what he told her. "You like this Romeo, for you are flattered to be the object of feelings on the part of such a handsome and gifted young man. However, what you take for his love is only his incessant effort to convince himself that he should love you. He even succeeds in this, because the games he plays with himself require it. So much I guess from his lifeline. Categorically I advise you not to enter into any durable union with him."

Of course, it did not help. What followed is too sad to compose into a story.

HUSBAND AND WIFE

She would not go to church because of her innate probity, which always pronounced itself clearly, yes-yes, no-no. Once inside, it was necessary to pretend to think and feel something one did not. Perhaps, also, she was a born rationalist, and the words as well as the actions of priests remained for her incomprehensible. If there is a God, he does not need these songs, incantations, and mumblings.

Her husband would go to church, submitting to the strong habits of his Catholic education, and if one Sunday he missed Mass, he felt like a little boy who had not done his homework. His motives, however, were rather equivocal. One could say that he was motivated as much by his sense of humor as by compassion. People (and he himself) appeared to him as too miserable to be exposed to demands in the name of pure reason. Under their aping and their incurable childishness was the expectation of a sudden unveiling of the absolute truth, but nothing of what they felt could be expressed and what was left was to repeat the words, gestures, and movements of the ritual. Every Sunday morning he plunged into thoughts about hidden bereavement, his own and theirs, while participating in a theater they created together that was comic, holy, and pitiful.

ALASTOR

It would be an exaggeration to say that the films directed by Alastor are gloomy, yet they are disquieting. They have their fans who appreciate in them precisely the ambiguity of the characters and the use made of symbols. Alastor's case is peculiar, as can be guessed not only from his films but also from his quite numerous pronouncements in interviews and articles.

A man of traumas and obsessions, Alastor simply declared that he did not like his films, because they were not positive enough. He would like to make different ones, but till now he did not know how. He confessed that he was a Christian but a sinner, and his personal shortcomings were responsible for what depressed him in his art, though there were also objective reasons for its defects.

To grow up in a pious Anglican family was not enough to preserve one's independence from the pressures of a milieu which did not care much for religion, and Alastor lived like his peers, perhaps differing from them only in his being given to philosophy. At a certain moment, however, he went through a crisis and the faith of his childhood recovered its lost meaning. This occurred not under the influence of any preachers but because of Tolkien's *The Lord of the Rings*, which he read in his adolescence and which worked slowly in him for years. A fairy tale about the struggle between good and evil, it suddenly tore him from his amused tolerance toward illusory standards of human moral judgments and threw him into a meditation on the power of evil in his century. Identifying ourselves with a hero from our adolescent readings, we often pave the way, unaware, for the decisions taken in maturity, and Alastor, like Frodo Baggins in Tolkien, came to feel that he was burdened with a mission to oppose the ominous land of Mordor.

Judging by many signs, Hell was spreading over the world like a drop of ink on blotting paper, and this was happening not only outside but also inside every one of his contemporaries. Alastor observed that dark stain in himself and in moments of soul-searching was ashamed of his life, so similar to that of his friends and acquaintances. Calling a spade a spade, he was a bigamist and an adulterer, which fact could help him in reaching the public, for he certainly was not old-fashioned, yet it was detrimental to his image of himself as a delegate of the forces of good, battling Mordor's dominion.

In his films a murderer is usually surprised that such a thing could happen to him. Me, so good and kind, how could I have done something like that? In such situations it was not difficult to see the director's efforts to cope with his own internal disorder, which he either excluded from moral judgment by special privilege or, reluctantly, submitted to the exigencies of the Ten Commandments.

What was the meaning of his speaking out against his films? His ideal was simplicity of action combined with the defeat of evil and the triumph of good, of the kind that appeals to children. Is it not true, he asked, that *The Magic Flute* is Bergman's best film, and is not this due to the music of Mozart? Yet in his striving toward his ideal of luminosity and simplicity Alastor stumbled upon an impassable barrier, as if built into the very technique of the genre he practiced. This astounded and angered him. He even began to suspect that, in a demonic century, works not contaminated by the darkness of Hell are possible as the rarest exceptions only.

A HISTORIAN'S WORRIES

Professor Theophilus, a historian, followed with sadness a successful campaign at the universities directed against the notion of objective truth. His Puritan ancestors, in the name of what they believed to be true, left the British Islands in the seventeenth century, and now he felt himself relegated to a quaintness as obstinate as theirs. A generation of scholars who in their youth had passed through Marxism, absorbed the writings of French theoreticians, and swore by the name of Nietzsche, had learned to sneer at truth as a shibboleth of metaphysicians and a mask of oppression.

Theophilus chose for the subject of his research, quite deliberately, a teeny district lost somewhere in the entrails of Europe, in order to avoid illusory generalizations and to discover what really did occur there during the Second World War. Seemingly, nothing deserving attention could happen there: a couple of small towns, villages, marshes, and forests. In fact, a solid knowledge of the past was indeed necessary simply to understand how it came about that such a small area had seen, during the war, people speaking five languages and professing several religions. Silence and the somewhat melancholy beauty of this province (which he visited, to test his linguistic capabilities) seemed to extol the power of forgetting. Yet it was enough to pull one thread of testimony to make emerge, one after another, images more terrible than those invented by the fantasy of even the most sadistic painters. People were beaten, raped, executed, hung, buried alive, stoned, kicked when wounded till they died. No pain that can be experienced by the human body was spared them.

But who was killing, who was raping, who was torturing? Who was an executioner and who was a victim? Stones in this region would not say anything, tombs had not been marked, grass long ago covered the hastily dug graves. One of the honorable traits of men is their will to leave their reports as witnesses. Some testimonies and memoirs survived, but Theophilus discovered that they contradicted one another. The same event in town X appeared differently in every description, depending upon the nationality of the witness and his native tongue. Theophilus put much effort into sifting material, only to conclude that a clear-cut assigning of responsibility was impossible and that every party would be able to invoke circumstances presumably justifying their behavior.

Yet children grew, born when that past had already turned into misty legend. They learned about the crimes, which, however, were always presented in such a way that the perpetrators were never "us," always "them." In neighboring schools, different in the language used for teaching, the children learned that "we" (the same as the other children's "they") would never lower ourselves to do the things our enemies accuse us of doing.

Theophilus, though conceding that his obstinate search for the true version of events produced only partially satisfactory results, nevertheless thought that the mockers who derided the notion of truth should cover themselves with a blush of shame. Enclosed in their labyrinths of theory, with which they obtained doctorates and jobs, they would not admit that their delight in being detractors might have practical consequences. It was enough for one or two individuals influenced by them to renounce investigating truth in history, and generations of children would be fed inventions, concocted for the most transient political purposes.

TALE OF A HERO

Many men earned the name of hero thanks to their solidarity with their comrades in arms. A minimum of personal self-respect required that they not let one another down in danger. Besides, brotherhood grew naturally between persons who felt and thought the same way. Quite different was the case of a young man whom we may call Caius, to avoid speculation. Filled with traumas and internal wounds, he distanced himself from his peers, as they, in his opinion, would reject him because of his origins. In his school years his mistrustful character was marked by the melancholy of a lonely child. Endowed with ambition to be the first in his class, he got good grades and this protected him in part, though his aloofness was evident. In reality, his feeling toward his classmates was a kind of amused scorn. Nevertheless, when the time of the ultimate test came during the war, he did not hesitate and, together with them, joined a clandestine armed resistance group, though the thought of his probable death at their side was difficult for him to accept. He did not appraise as high the chances of survival, either for himself or for other soldiers of the underground, and for months he cultivated a thorny tree of meditations on the theme of sacrifice. The further he was from the ideas and impulses of his comrades, the greater seemed to him the sacrifice he was certain he must assume out of his feeling of duty. When he was killed in action, his courage made him a legendary figure, yet no biographer of his would dare suspect in him this hidden struggle.

ON A DESERT ISLAND

How difficult it would be today to write *Robinson Crusoe*! The hero of the novel, when he found himself on a desert island, was incessantly active, trying to arrange his life as best he could. A new Robinson would probably sit and think, with the worst possible results. So in any case we must presume, judging by the general inclination of literature to introspection as well as to narratives in the first-person singular.

A man on a desert island has to confront the basic fact of a lack of communication with other living beings; he talks in vain to fish, crabs, and birds. That is, he is hit in what is most human: he loses speech. The other Robinson had at least a parrot and taught it a few words, but that was meager conversation. The hopeless position of a castaway consists in his realizing that everything in him came from people; i.e., people residing in his mind. Their disappearance leaves him defenseless before empty time which just flows. His situation resembles somewhat that of a prisoner in a solitary cell, though he is better off, for he can run, swim, and warm himself in the sun. Yet he is worse off, because outside the cell are his jailers, who are responsible for his misfortune and with whom he quarrels in his thoughts, while on the island he is surrounded only by the sea and the sky. He is given over to rummaging in his past, no longer controlled by "now." True, monks—eremites who of their own free will choose the desert or a solitary cave in the wilderness—could live without people, but they were sustained by prayer, which is a conversation with God. If that vertical bond weakened, they fell victim to acedia, a demon of boredom, and the absurd.

How could present-day writers, trained in noting down their perceptions and memories, write of a solitary character otherwise than by examining his "states of consciousness"? Robinson Crusoe, fortunately for himself, had no time: not only had he to stave off hunger, but his thoughts were constantly suggesting to him useful work, improvements, to be carried out soon, the next day. Since the seventeenth century we have advanced in losing our sense of hierarchy, which assigns first place to what is simplest.

A RED UMBRELLA

Looking at a landscape, we may think that only we change and the landscape remains the same. This is not true; it preserves its shape for no more than one or two generations. Earthly time has its regularities. The trees grow, and the ground, once open to the sun, is now in shade. Wet lowlands are left by a flood, with vegetation different from before; a storm topples old giants and young thickets shoot up—but pines, not hornbeams. Yet the greatest changes are introduced by human time. Memory may preserve a spruce forest, but no trace of it can be found; even the stumps left after the felling have been cleared. The eye searches for clusters of green, for orchards of apple, pear, and plum trees, among which there should be roofs of huts, of barns, and cowsheds. But nothing of that has survived, the orchards have been cut, buildings burned down, and now we have before us a flat expanse of fields right up to the horizon, to be plowed by a tractor.

Through that country, let us assume, the spirit of the heiress walks with her red umbrella. To the valid objection that spirits do not carry umbrellas, one may answer that something, after all, must happen to the multitude of departed and useless objects, only some of which find their way to antique shops. So Miss Lilka or Isia walks there, the one who once was fond of l'art nouveau and who frequented the literary cabarets of 1900. She realizes that something incongruous took place here, as we should be able to return to the places of our youth in the hope that even if they are changed, they could still be recognized. She looks for the manor's park, but sees only the scrub and hollows of a wasteland. She examines a spot overgrown with burdocks and thistles and says to herself that this must have been the arbor where she and Witold embraced. It is strange, she thinks, that everything is gone, no park, no arbor, but what is even more strange, in my wanderings through the beyond I have never met Witold, which probably means that I never loved him.

THE SECRET OF CATS

Cats have cohabited with humans for millennia and to all appearances there is no mystery in it. Pleading their cause, they could invoke centuries of faithful service. Agricultural civilizations meant grain, and where there is grain, there are mice. Then conditions changed, but the cats stayed on.

And yet it is worthwhile to ponder a peculiarity of the cat's office. Have you not noticed the expression of playfulness and jocular interest on the faces of our fellow men as soon as we start to talk about cats? Something similar immediately animates faces if the conversation moves to sex. As to dogs, they do not provoke such reflexes of half-secret but familiar connivance. I maintain that, after all, humans and cats are bound by a fleshly agreement and no one of us behaves toward a cat in his or her capacity as a person, but simply as a physical being, surrendering to the senses of sight and touch, the senses that attract us to certain trees, flowers, birds, animals, landscapes, to certain shapes and colors. The cat by its very appearance calls for touching and stroking; hence, in the language of love, those innumerable cajoling expressions, those kitties, kittens, and pussies. Moreover, our senses of sight and touch, confronted with a cat, act the same way, whether we are a child, an old man, a male, or a female. Love of cats, cruelties inflicted on cats, seem to be two sides of one attraction, common to young and old.

This universality deserves meditation. Notwithstanding the particular features of every individual, we belong to the same species, possess its head, its hands and legs; an anatomical atlas shows what we carry inside. Also, we are so constructed that just as a sunflower turns its face toward the sun, we turn toward things to which we give the names of beautiful and nice. And so, as soon as we grant a moment of attention to our erotic (oh yes!) predilection for the cat, we start asking ourselves questions about nothing less than the permanent traits in our nature.

The more so because a cat nature undoubtedly exists, and our pact with the cat signifies a meeting of its and our nature. But consciousness, but language, but history!—they would exclaim, how far from this poor animal to all that! Let us not puff ourselves up with pride and let us not separate the high regions of our spirit from elementary sensations. Rather, let us profit from the presence of a member of our household who right now is stretched on an armchair, and let us try to forget about the arguments of philosophers of our century who assure us that there is no human nature. If it is difficult to defend its existence, in the face of the river of change that does not spare anything, at least here, before this creature who yawns and shows the tip of its rosy tongue, the durability of my own nature in me, who looks at it with sympathy, is beyond doubt. And—let me stress it—it is not irrelevant whether human nature exists or not. Only if it exists, may we attempt to establish which among our laws and institutions are good for it, which are detrimental and contrary to its basic needs.

Thus, from cats to a big philosophical problem. Even if they are not aware of it, we may ascribe to their presence among us our awareness, modest enough, after all, of our place.

COMING UNGLUED

What I am going to say will be understood by those of us who have lived such a moment: for instance, during a historical upheaval, when the life of a human society suddenly reveals its unsuspected traits. Since there have been in this century a number of historical upheavals, many people have had the experience.

It happens that we may walk, watch, be tormented by our compassion or anger, and suddenly realize that what we are seeing, all that reality, is beyond words. That is, there is nothing about it in newspapers, books, communiqués, nothing in poetry, fiction, or pictures on the screen. From reality which is homely, perceived in a most ordinary way, something else, autonomous, enclosed in language, has come unglued. Astonished, we ask ourselves: Is it a dream? A fata morgana? The fabric of signs envelops us like a cocoon and proves to be strong enough to make us doubt the testimony of our senses.

Such an experience does not incline us favorably toward literature. It compels us to ask for realism, which usually leads to pseudorealism or for a veracity nobody could bear. In the nineteenth century it was said about the novel that it should be a "mirror carried on the highway," but "realistic" novels lied without scruple, clearing from the field of vision subjects recognized as undesirable or forbidden. The true London of nineteenth-century capitalism hardly exists in the novel, except for a few pages of Dickens, but what that Babylon of misery and prostitution was, seen through the eyes of a foreigner in 1862, we may learn from Dostoevsky's *Winter Notes on Summer Impressions.*

The twentieth century brought with it a fictitious reality fashioned by the political will. It was a screen, painted with "scenes from life" to hide what was going on in back. It was called socialist realism. Yet the orders and prohibitions of the state are only one of the possible causes of this division into the seen and the described. The fabric of language has a constant propensity to come off from reality, and our efforts to glue them together are in most cases futile—yet absolutely necessary.

TABOO

Taboo, i.e., "not allowed," was the foundation of the feudal system on the islands of Polynesia and consisted in recognizing certain persons (for instance, chiefs and priests) as well as some places and objects as untouchable. Because of Dr. Freud and his successors, we learned to associate the word "taboo" with sex, yet the islanders had no idea that some bodily functions could be forbidden. This became in Hawaii a significant factor in the encounter with the white man's civilization. A young British sailor, Thomas Manby, who found himself in Hawaii in 1791, describes (with relish) a group of girls on the deck of his ship—they got there in canoes or by swimming and stayed for a few days. When Protestant missionaries appeared in Honolulu, they were particularly severe toward this custom, and there were scandals when ship captains requested entertainment for their crews.

When, in a few dozen years, the taboo, the violation of which was punished by death, gradually disappeared on the Hawaiian Islands, it was equivalent to the end of their civilization, and the (awful) Protestant missionaries confronted a society in a state of utter decay, without any orientation as to how to live. They introduced the notion of sin, and it encompassed not only sex but also dances and games, for which the penalty was Hell.

The history of our civilization is a history of changing taboos. In our century, utopias such as the Soviet state used the taboo to protect themselves, and the gradual disintegration of prohibitions was a sign that what had happened to Hawaiian feudalism would repeat itself there.

The breaking of barriers in a "permissive society" is limited mainly to sex, not without comic efforts to discover sexual acts drastic enough to boost sales. Freedom seems to be total and thus numerous taboos in other realms are beyond people's awareness.

I boast of being aware of taboos which are binding in the place and time assigned to my life. It is better, I feel, to be aware than to submit unconsciously. Sometimes I have an itch to test how much freedom is allowed, but I stifle this urge for various reasons. What those taboos are, I prefer not to reveal; I would expose myself too much. Other people, in the proper season, which is not the season of my life, will take care of that.

The gods of ancient Greece were capricious. Human fates depended upon their will, yet humans had a hard time trying to guess what would gain the gods' favor, what would provoke their anger. Then those inhabitants of the heavens, who from time to time walked the earth, disappeared, together with the nymphs of mountain springs, the dryads of old trees, and the sirens of the seas. Their return, after many centuries of exile, was not probable. And yet the return occurred, at least in books, such as a book by a certain eminent cosmologist, Sebastian Kuo.

Considering that the Creator of the universe had already lost much of His authority in the eighteenth century, when He was magnanimously granted the title of the Great Clockmaker who, once having put machinery in motion, did not meddle with its functioning; considering that the terrible suffering of people in the ensuing centuries, provoked by wars and genocide, made interventions by Providence seem even less probable; considering, finally, that the human mind learned to link the notion of scientific truth with empirical proof—cosmologists attempting to find out how the universe came into being carefully avoided any ideas that would suggest their affiliation with religion. Some scientists, though, wondering at the precision of the laws governing matter after the Big Bang, were not loath to postulate the existence of powerful intelligences which act in a manner incomprehensible to us, possibly for their own amusement. One of these men of science, Sebastian Kuo, even expressed the opinion that our universe might be their experiment based upon quantum mechanics, or even a simulation. His book, however—which, he himself concedes, is on the border of science fiction—has for its primary subject our life on earth and examines the highly enigmatic role in it of chance and coincidence. We are inclined—goes the argument—to intuit a logic behind events which we can almost grasp, yet it eludes us and we are sentenced to ignorance again. Should we not imagine two teams, endowed with intelligence inaccessible to us, engaged in a sort of game of chess, using us as if we were symbols in a computer? This would explain the entanglements of our fates, meetings which it is hard to call haphazard, misfortunes falling on us when we least expect them, successes acquiring ironic meaning. This also would explain glimpses of logic in our personal histories, so that we are inclined sometimes to believe in Fatum, when a sudden departure from regularity occurs, when obviously another hand has entered the game. What the Greeks told themselves about the gods' councils, loves, and mutual enmities, on which the adventures

of mortals depended, was clever, for it proved—reasons the
scientist—that they had an intuitive grasp of the distance sep-
arating our will from a higher sort of calculation, indifferent
to our desires and laments.

LESS AND LESS CONFESSIONS

The Jesuit had lenses so thick that I could not guess from his eyes whether his words expressed irony or the zeal of a polemicist.

"Yes, in many countries the institution of confession tends to disappear," he said. "In a parish where the Masses are full, hardly five or ten people a month go to confession. And those who do go expect qualifications which I, at least, do not have. After all, I have no training in psychiatry.

"A man came to me once and told me in advance that he wanted to reveal the greatest crime of his life. This proved to be the killing of a bird. A small bird that flew in through an open window. The man did not know much about birds. Friends to whom he described it decided it might have been a kind of grosbeak, but not European, so probably it was kept by somebody in a cage. It might have been an African sparrow or something of the sort. The man bought a cage and put grain out for the bird, but it did not want to eat yet it looked as if it were dying of hunger. 'Then, with the best of intentions,' the man told me, 'I tried to open its beak and put in a bit of softened bread, but it resisted and gave a strange quiver in my hand. I tried again, but when I opened its beak by force, it quivered, fluttered, and died. I realized that it had had a heart attack, out of fright.' "

The priest asked the man why he considered this so heavy a crime. He was told that the event acquired for the man a symbolic dimension and explained how he became responsible for the death of a human being. Without realizing it, and with the best of intentions, he behaved like a tyrant toward a woman with whom he had lived. He was unable to understand that someone could think differently from him and appraise various matters and people differently. For her good he would argue that she was wrong and advise her to change her behavior. She took it badly, interpreting his insistence as a personal attack. Such, even involuntary, harshness, the man maintained, is given at divorce trials the name of "mental cruelty." Their union ended, and soon after that, she died. There was a suspicion of suicide.

From behind the thick glasses, there was an enigmatic glance. "They concoct a story and come to the confessional with it. That man, for example, out of guilt, put events together in an obviously obsessive way, and we can't really know what was invented and what wasn't. Or what got left out. Seemingly, we are supposed to give absolution for fantasies that people have created, either to magnify their sins or so that we will not become aware of the sins they really have committed."

A PRIEST AND CASANOVA

Cardinal Giannini liked the scoundrel, whom he had met at a time when, still wearing a cassock, the young man served as secretary to Cardinal Aquaviva. And, later on, he liked to follow news of the international career of his former protégé, who now proclaimed himself a master of the occult arts. In a library adorned with friezes painted by Giulio Romano, the cardinal worked on a theological treatise, behind the words of which the unnamed lurked, and the unnamed owed something to his meditation on the spectacle of human lives such as Casanova's.

In his youth, Giannini was a lover of the theater and also, which is inevitable, of theater dressing rooms, with their secrets of powder and rouge, their rows of multicolored wigs on the walls, and mirrors in which the light of candles trembled.

Son of an itinerant actress, Casanova was regarded by theater troupes as one of their own, and, of course, he transformed life into a commedia dell'arte, full of masks, magical incantations, tarot cards, and curative elixirs. To what order did he belong, then? the cardinal asked himself. The division of the world into two orders was for him obvious. One, constantly created anew by human thought, seemed to soar a few inches above the ground and was attested to by the volumes of Saint Thomas

Aquinas on the library shelves, by the cupolas designed by Bramante, by the Bernini colonnade, by the paintings of Michelangelo and Raphael, but also by the work of the laborer, the soldier, the merchant, the diplomat. For many people, however, that was only the order of appearances, for they, these men and women, gave themselves with ardor to something else. They resided in a realm where a look, a seemingly accidental brushing of one's hand, a bumping against each other in a corridor, are meaningful—and their meaning is always the same. In that game of secret invitations and signals, women were most skilled; women, Gozzi said, from their twelfth year had only one thing on their minds. Casanova knew how to read signs and his one-man enterprise of amorous rescue service worked faultlessly, whether with maidens, wives, or widows. And it would be wrong to call him a seducer, for he merely responded, like a swimmer borne by a wave.

In that order, scruples did not count, neither a notion of sin nor the fear of Hell; the mind trained itself in inventing ruses, guiles, intrigues, disguises, always in the service of the same endeavor, so there was no help in doors locked by a jealous husband, iron bars in the windows of a maiden's room, not even in isolation in a tower without a staircase. The cardinal was amused by the lightness of touch in Casanova's craft and, returning in his thoughts to his own youth, almost envied him.

For he had known, after all, that course of days and nights when we live in the uninterrupted bliss of amorous promise. He renounced all that, and, old now, pored over his books, asking himself a question.

This order he served by moving his pen over paper, what was it? If to don the robe of a sorcerer or of a king, to hide under a wig one's true hair color, and to pretend to be somebody else, is the very essence of theater, this order of his was a big spectacle in several acts. Except that it lacked the moment when the curtain goes down and the actresses and actors crowd into dressing rooms, taking off their robes, sashes, and pantaloons, washing off color from their faces, and rushing to taverns. Obviously, the roles have been assigned, but who hid behind them could hardly be guessed: beings of that second order, unstable, mortal, always on the move, fleeing danger or pursuing pleasure. Had Casanova been only a rake and a swindler, the thing would not have offered food for thought. He displayed such a liking for hazard and adventure, however, that his horoscopes, his sword thrusts, his jumping from a height into the sea to escape from a fortress, and even his nights of card playing when gold talers lay heaped on the table beside him, fulfilled in abundance the requirements of the theatrical. Stretching between amorous pursuits and the fantasies that intensified their charm, his life reminded Giannini of the carnal passion present in all works of the human mind and hand, and warned against withdrawing into high regions of abstraction. The cardinal wrote, and syllogisms displayed themselves under his pen, and against philosophers too certain of the power of pure reason he would put: *sed contram.*

DICTIONARY

The town in which they have lived for many years had a plant that provided employment for many of its inhabitants. Gedrus and Gerdra worked there long enough to acquire a small house and a modest social security pension. They were a well-matched married couple, though without children. Liked by their neighbors, they shared with them their joys and sorrows: the illumination of streets and houses at Christmas, a flood when turgid waters nearly reached the edge of town, complaints about high taxes, marriages and funerals.

There was something, however, that made them different from the rest of their fellow citizens; namely, they spoke between themselves a language nobody in the town knew, except them. They came as immigrants from a faraway small country, which they had left in their adolescence, but its landscapes remained vivid in their memory and returned with every word they uttered in their own tongue. Only the mailman, who lived on the same street, was aware of their peculiarity, since he incessantly brought them books and newspapers with titles impossible to pronounce.

The idea was born in his, perhaps in her, head—in any case both found it excellent. They were just retiring, so they could dedicate all their time to a task which was to fulfill, as they unanimously said, the greatest love of their lives. Imagine: they decided to create a dictionary, so that their native tongue would appear in all its beauty and strength. Rejecting the argument that, after all, dictionaries already existed, they explained to themselves their unique method, which consisted in grouping words into units depending on the affinity of their roots.

In the beginning, when they had hardly started, they realized the immensity of the enterprise and they asked themselves whether it could be completed within the limited time left to them by old age. They put aside other occupations, even renounced the raising of rabbits, and every morning they set to work and stayed at it late into the night.

Slowly they plodded onward year after year and they never felt so close to each other and so happy. They loved not only words but also the intonations they remembered from their native village, just as they remembered rural labors, tools, seasons, and since all that was dear to both of them, every day they grew in mutual understanding.

It took them six years, but when the dictionary was ready, its huge size precluded their finding a publisher. So they decided to establish their own publishing house, Gedrus and Gerdra, to copy the whole onto a computer, print it, and bind it. They advertised in émigré newspapers for subscriptions, which, o wonder, found enough reponse to cover the cost of the volume, so substantial that its thickness nearly equals its length and width.

Pronouncements of specialists on this work testify rather to a respect for the labor involved than to the service it rendered to linguistics; their self-invented method seems to have some weak points. Nevertheless, even the most reluctant concede that no lover of that little-known tongue will be able to bypass a monument erected for its glory by the old couple.

LOVE OF KNOWLEDGE

In his school years Victor considered himself superior to his classmates, for he took an interest in so-called serious problems. He tried to read difficult books, though he did not boast by mentioning their titles, afraid of being mocked; he persisted in that reading to impress only himself. Toward the end of high school, he even bought the *Ethics* of Spinoza, but put it down after a few pages, for he did not understand a word.

At the university, he chose a branch of studies that he judged prestigious enough for an individual of exceptional qualities. Dropping nonchalantly the name of his specialty when asked would help him considerably to stay in a good frame of mind.

We do not hesitate to assert that Victor was a snob, for, after all, what is snobbery if not adding a little to one's height in one way or another? Some are proud of their ancestors, others of their wealth, whereas Victor saw himself in the robes of a scholar and strutted on the stilts of pretended wisdom.

Whatever his ideas about himself, his diligence could not be doubted. Laboriously he plodded through abstruse books and, encountering unknown words, reached for dictionaries. Gradually the contents of those books, read attentively, were becoming clearer, and he acquired considerable competence, especially as he learned to use his time economically.

We should add that he admired his own sharp intelligence, which justified, in his opinion, the high regard in which he held his own person, even if this was not kindly received by others.

A certain inevitable discovery he made influenced his career; namely, he noticed that there was a gap between what one *should* know and what one *can* know. The quantity of theories, hypotheses, trends, names, papers, was so vertiginous that only a superhuman mind would have been able to cope with it. Thus, the initiated observed a tacit agreement: that they would not be held responsible for actually reading the works of celebrities whose names they liked to invoke, and that the mention of these names meant that they had mastered a professional language. That language allowed them to move amid the plethora, in the same way that a man crosses a river by jumping from one ice floe to another. As Victor became aware of this, he stopped using his energy to collect information and concentrated on mastering the language. From that moment on, he advanced quickly.

———

Already as an assistant professor Victor won renown first within his department, then in wider and wider circles. Appointed a full professor, he increased the prestige of his university by attending numerous international seminars and symposiums.

When he died in a plane accident, two of his old classmates took part in the funeral of the great man. One was a dentist, and one was a farmer. They did not claim to like Victor, but they respected learning and this led them to ask themselves certain questions afterward over a drink. In order to become a famous man, was it necessary, as early as one's childhood, to turn one's back on people, as Victor had done? To scorn them? To sacrifice everything to the achievement of one goal? And what goal? Is it, they wondered impartially, a disinterested love of knowledge? And what does that mean?

TALE OF A CONVERT

A certain man, Paul by name, had never reflected on the meaning of his having been baptized in childhood, and of his filling the blank space for religious denomination: "Roman Catholic."

Till, as a result of a painful experience in his personal life, he began to believe in God. Then he decided to take an interest in religion. He bought a catechism and started to read. Here is what he found there.

1. God is the creator of all things, visible and invisible. Before He created the world, He created incorporeal beings endowed with intelligence and free will, whom the Holy Writ calls messengers; that is, angels. The relationship of God to those beings was similar to that, later on, of God to man.

2. Evil and suffering have their origin in the fall of some of the angels, who by an act of free will chose to adore themselves instead of adoring their Creator.

3. The creation of the world is identical with the beginning of time. Submitted to time, life on earth—vegetation, fish, birds,

animals—created by God was recognized by Him as good. Nature existed under the rule of laws different from those of today.

4. God created man as a being second only to angels. He made him perfect, saintly and, though corporeal, not subject to old age and death.

5. In the earthly Paradise, where he placed man, there was a Tree of Knowledge, the fruit of which man should not eat, so as not to bring death on himself. By an act of free will, man broke this prohibition, succumbing to the temptation of a fallen angel, that is, the devil, and for a similar reason: he wanted to adore himself and not his Creator. By that act he brought death on the whole of humankind, but also upon Nature, which underwent a change in its laws. How this Sin, called Original, can burden all humans living since is a mystery which cannot be fathomed.

6. Original Sin did not merely provide a bad example, as was affirmed by Pelagius, nor did it spoil human nature irrevocably, as Protestants of the sixteenth century maintained, but it changed human nature, making it susceptible to evil actions, which inclination is called *concupiscentia*; i.e., desire.

———

7. Without Original Sin there would have been no Incarnation; that is, God would not have taken the shape of man in Christ, who is a victor over death and all evil, both in fallen angels and in man. This catastrophe in Creation, a consequence of decisions made by beings endowed with free will, provoked God's intervention in the history of mankind and His revelation of Himself to Moses and to the prophets, and then his descent to the earth in the shape of Christ.

8. The mystery of the preconceived Son who is both God and man, who died on the cross and rose from the dead, i.e., the mystery of the Holy Trinity, is the very foundation of the Roman Catholic religion. It means that God is not an indifferent giver of laws of the universe, but that He is Providence, who cares about the history of humans.

9. God reveals Himself in the inspired books of the Old and of the New Testament, and, as the Holy Spirit, He leads his people, so that they preserve the truth. The sending of the Holy Spirit also opens the history of the Universal, Catholic, and Apostolic Church.

Paul, underlining in the catechism words and sentences, was astounded and terrified. For what he read there had nothing in common with the way people of the twentieth century thought and, in fact, was just the opposite. Instead of a Cosmos inexorably moving by itself, its laws were made dependent upon the error of living creatures, invisible and visible. Instead of life blindly progressing from one-cell organisms to more and more complex ones, till the emergence of manlike mammals and then of man, a primeval perfection was postulated, as well as a Fall, bringing about the fall of everything alive. Yet without the Fall there would not have been any need for the Saviour, nor a promise of the kingdom at the end of time, when Nature returns to its primal glory and death is no more.

If I am a Catholic, I should believe in all this? Paul asked himself, and delved in the Letters of his namesake, the great man whose incomprehensible energy had built up the Church.

It's really hard, but since I believe in God, I have no way out, and my very gratitude to Him compels me to accept the credo of my denomination. Unless I try to elaborate my own religion. But who am I to come forth against the two millennia during which generation after generation shared this faith?

Paul, however, did not stop at this reasoning but attempted to reflect on its consequences. People of the past showed through their works that they treated the truth of their faith seriously. They painted many representations of angels and some even dared to imagine devilish figures. The greatest—and the longest—literary works had for their subject Salvation and Damnation—Dante's *Divine Comedy*, Milton's *Paradise Lost*, Goethe's *Faust*.

The horror felt by Paul was understandable, for suddenly he realized that mankind had entered a new phase, in which the notions of transgression and punishment, of Salvation and Damnation, had disappeared. More and more people did not believe in anything, even in the truth of science. But in what did the faithful who filled churches and recited prayers in various tongues believe? They confessed a mollified religion in which the main rule seemed to be "it may be so, but it may be otherwise" and in which everybody picked out what in his opinion was believable.

Paul's heart asked for truth. One truth which could not be different a thousand years or five hundred years ago and which, for everyone who would cling to it, would be binding.

If, according to the multitude of signs, modern civilization was the scene of the activity of the Tempter, called also the Father of Lies and the Prince of This World, a Christian's duty was to oppose him.

———

Paul realized that caution advised marching in step with others; namely, assuming that Christianity was a huge charity association headed by the noblest of the preachers, Jesus, who followed in the footsteps of Buddha. And also in dismissing as metaphors those teachings of the Church which to the minds of his contemporaries seemed outlandish and unacceptable.

Against common sense, Paul ceased to behave as others did and so laid the foundations for a universally shared opinion of his weirdness. He declared that he believed in angels and devils; moreover, he violently condemned some books and films, branding them as inspired by the evil spirit. He also antagonized some powerful personalities, reproaching them with the demoniac activity of demoralizers. His participation in protests against pornography and against certain varieties of music earned him the name of enemy of everything that is new.

He fared no better in personal matters, for, desiring to follow the teachings of the Church, he proposed marriage to Ivonne, with whom he lived, and this proposal was not well received, for Ivonne wanted to pursue her professional career and marriage was associated in her mind with child-bearing.

Poor Paul earned only a sad notoriety and at the mention of his name people would, with a wobbling finger, make a little circle at their temple. He complained to his confessor, who, though respectful of Paul's probity, did not completely approve of his direct attacks on the Adversary, without due consideration for strategy and tactics. According to the priest, the folly which fell upon humanity could not be lasting, as this would contradict God's promise given to His Church. As long as it is here, however, the faithful should be advised to observe a reasonable pliability and even a certain discretion in revealing their convictions.

What happened to Paul next? Reports from the circles he frequented differ. Here are the gathered materials.

Jack:

Paul did not follow his confessor's advice. He found another solution. Since he had acquired among his acquaintances the reputation of a crackpot, he looked for like-minded souls and he found many. In fact, there was a whole movement, not quite backed by the Church hierarchy yet sufficiently strong to enlist a considerable part of the clergy and of the faithful under the banner of conservatism. Liberated from the feeling of impropriety—on the contrary, lauded and admired—Paul engaged himself in the League that took for its aim to implement Catholic values in the life of society through legislation. In a short time, he became one of the leaders of a political party that fought for a law forbidding abortion and divorce. He did not doubt that his campaign against Evil was necessary, even if he was shocked by some pronouncements of his allies, who went rather far in their abuse of liberals. He would bear with it, though, in the name of the primary goal.

His political activity hurt his private life, thus confirming the dependence of physical harmony between a couple upon the harmony of their minds. Ivonne did not have kind words for the League and for his party, and was even inclined to condemn them violently, saying, "You want to save human lives, but you destroy human souls," which meant that, according to her, many young people were abandoning religion, as they identified it with campaigns of hatred launched by the League's militants. More and more apart from each other, Paul and Ivonne were less a couple than a marriage torn by quarrels and misunderstandings, till at last they decided to separate.

Therese:
That's not how it happened. Paul looked for people who thought like him, but, given the circles he landed in, it was as if he had followed exactly the counsels of his confessor. These circles were mostly convinced that, in view of the advances of consumer society, resistance was futile, and Catholics could do no more than practice a delaying action, while preserving the

appearance of being in harmony with the world. The Church had been right to excommunicate Voltaire, for "permissive" patterns had their origin in the Enlightenment, yet the progress of science, technology, medicine, which followed from that time, was too useful to allow for condemnation of the entire Enlightenment heritage. Paul meditated upon mass culture as a possible means to convince people they acted for their own destruction. They were in the grip of *concupiscentia*, desire, desire of money, power, and sex, but you could not reach them except by pretending to be one of them, for otherwise they turned their backs on you. So how to speak to them? Through images; i.e., through films. For that reason Paul started to make movies, the kind that might be successful, with situations well known to the public and the requisite and unavoidable amount of nakedness. The message was in the action yet so discreetly that critics were unable to agree on its meaning.

The union of Paul and Ivonne went through innumerable complications, which ended in her getting pregnant, after which they married.

Steve:

It was totally different from that. After his first flights as a moralist, which earned him the reputation of a crank, Paul grew ashamed and realized that from his reading of the cathechism he had drawn wrong conclusions. Whatever the causes of evil, the very essence of the world consists in the suffering of man and of all living creatures. To live means to be stigmatized by death and it is precisely this unavoidable fact which lies at the core of Christianity. Thus, at the center of our reflexions should be, not punishment and merit, but man's weakness, so great that it deserves the greatest pity and, indeed, it inspired the cosmic pity of God. In the very order of things, in the chain of cause and effect, Paul detected diabolic signs, yet he recognized his error, for he should not have obsessively kept his attention tuned to a dark force which had spoiled and continued to spoil the good plan of the Creator. The flaw seemed to reside at the very core of life, and the Fall that occurred before the creation of time did not change it. The only real thing was the misfortune of people, their desperate calls to which no voice in the entire universe responded, and precisely this silence of the universe had to reach its full measure, so that divine Compassion responded by incarnating Itself in man and his history.

Paul was now inclined to ascribe his excessive concern with the moral disorder of his contemporaries to the influence of the Adversary, who, though without hooves and tail, knew how to take on various shapes, so why should he not appear in the cloak of a moralist? The faces of some preachers, distorted by hatred, proved this, and Paul, in order to repair his previous inclination to condemn, joined the Catholics called moderate, who, though they remained faithful to the Church *magisterium*, were accused of pernicious tolerance and of weakening the opposition to widely spread heresies. He became a polemicist and because of his pronouncements was attacked by persons who considered themselves to be better Catholics. They used arguments pertaining to his private life, mainly to his union, out of wedlock, with Ivonne.

Ivonne, as a result of Paul's activity, was incorporated, as she used to say, into a gang of believers, but she liked his colleagues and friends, felt accepted, and a bit teasingly would drop from time to time a remark that she was not in a hurry to marry.

Agnes:
What a crazy idea! After all, Paul did not live alone and every day he was exposed to the personality of Ivonne. While he had practically never been exposed to the lessons of religion, she had received a Catholic education and was making a specific use of it. She tried to attend Mass every Sunday, because there the community ascended together to the realm of the sacred, inaccessible to reason. She had not paid attention, though, to the sermons, which she dismissed as Alice in Wonderland tales. She regarded continuous attention paid to morals, especially to

sex, as detrimental to the vertical striving in religion. She rejected the threat of damnation after death, for, as she would say, people suffer so much on earth that there is no need for them to be tormented in an afterlife. Heaven was to her rather irrelevant, as she did not expect a reward for her good deeds and preferred not to be conscious of them. She never engaged in theological meditations on the origin of evil and simply confessed that she did not understand anything of those stories of devils and angels. She considered herself a Catholic, but in her own way; i.e., she believed the Church would one day recognize that she and others of her ilk were right. Agreeing with the Church authorities as to the philosophical seriousness of the problem of abortion, she had no intention of submitting to the prohibition against using contraceptives, and she would mock the rhythm method, asking how it differed from scientific methods that produced the pill. She also held her own opinions on Church organization, declaring herself in favor, though not too strongly, of women's priesthood.

Thus Paul had at home this world from the end of the second millennium against which he was supposed to protest. It looked as if he, in his zeal of a convert, would get unnecessarily agitated, while near him the so-called ordinary faithful quietly submitted to the ritual, the same for generations, getting along quite well without a logical doctrine. To see in this the decline of Christianity showed little common sense and perhaps a lack of trust in Providence. For there was the possibility of an enormous transformation, of which such thinking as Ivonne's could be a sign.

Paul renounced what, for some time, he had regarded as his mission and joined the crowd of ordinary mortals entering a church building every Sunday. This did not happen because of reasoning, however. It was caused by tenderness. Her long eyelashes, the attentive inclination of her head when she listened to music, states of despondency and of enthusiasm, her sinful ambition and goodwill.

A PHILOSOPHER

That philosopher was an atheist; i.e., he would not seek in the existence of the universe any signs indicating its first cause. The hypotheses of science managed without it, and he, though he had some doubts as to its methods, relied on them to learn about the nature of things. To be fair, we should add that even though he esteemed science, he did not belong to those dreamers who expect that reason would allow human beings to build a perfect society one day.

The only preoccupation worthy of a philosopher was, in his view, meditating on the meaning of religion. When reproached with contradicting himself, he would answer that man is a self-contradictory being, and thus he, in his pronouncements on the importance of religion, was in harmony with his humanity.

All splendor and all the dignity of man was contained, according to him, in religion. The very fact that so miserable a creature, so irrevocably mortal, was able to create good and evil, up and down, heavens and abysses, seemed to him incomprehensible and deserving of constant astonishment. Nowhere in the whole immense universe—not to be encompassed by imagination—was there even a shred of good, of pity, of compassion, and the questions prompted by the needs of the human heart found no response. The faithful of the chief religions of mankind did not, felt the philosopher, pay enough attention to the absolute loneliness of human consciousness under the starry sky. Even less inclined to reflect on this were followers of various shamanisms, who humanized Nature and blurred the borderline between the human and the animal kingdom.

The philosopher had a hard time coping with the idea of beauty ruled by the goddess Venus; i.e., by the force of Nature itself. He wrote a book to prove that beauty exists only where shapes and colors called to life by the goddess Venus encounter the sight and the hearing of man, two senses endowed with a magical power of transformation.

Not all religions were ranked the same by him. He assigned the highest place to those in which the opposition between man and the natural order of things was the most marked, in which, therefore, man by liberating himself from that order achieved salvation. In this respect, the first among them was Christianity; the next, Buddhism; for they both sanctified a trait exclusively human, compassion, against the stony face of the world. What could be more human than the God of Christianity, taking the shape of a man, and aware that the stony world would sentence Him to death? Because the Son reigned for eternity and in His name everything was created, it meant that the human shape and the human heart reside in the very bosom of God and suffer as they look at a world that was intended as good but was tainted by death because of the Fall.

The philosopher's respect turned first of all to the Roman, Catholic, and Apostolic Church, whose two millennia could suffice as an argument. In his century he witnessed furious attacks directed by the gates of Hell against that rock. Being a humanist, he should have rejoiced at the weakening of prohibitions that interfered with natural human desires; he, however, bowed his head before the Pope, who dared, openly and loudly, against the whole world, to proclaim "the sign of dissent."

Aware that civilization is threatened by decay if one truth does not provide it with a unifying bond, the philosopher in his public statements always sided with warnings flowing from the Vatican. He did not hide the fact that, though he was refused the grace of faith, he would like to be counted among the workers in the Lord's vineyard.

"We are allowed"—taking off her dress, the countess said to her lover, who, stretched on the bed, his head proppped on his elbow, observed her in the mirror. "Nevertheless, we should preserve appearances for the sake of the people"—she was loosening turtleshell combs from her masterful hairdo. "I have pangs of conscience because of my chambermaid Betsy, who, of course, does the same with her Joseph. Really, it's impossible to protect our servants; they simply live too close to their masters, so they watch and imitate. But there is that multitude of simple illiterate folk who continue to live in their villages in the way in which their grandfathers lived. It's terrifying to think what would have happened had every person looked at his or her betters and imagined himself or herself entitled to the same rights, money, and pleasures. You may call me a moralist, Zis, but it is enough to visualize a world in which all inhibitions are abolished. If we care for decency and good habits, it is only to protect them, those poor unfortunates, from themselves. Even though they aren't aware of it," she added, putting on a lace nightgown.

INSIDE AND OUTSIDE

We live inside and there is no help for it, just as the moles move daringly under the earth, while the airy outside, where the sun shines and birds fly, is for them an alien element. Or, to use another comparison, we live inside a leviathan which is referred to in words signifying interhuman activities: city, society, civilization, epoch. I once even imagined this interhuman creation as a gigantic cocoon hanging from the branch of a cosmic tree. Be that as it may, we reside inside, though in a better position than the moles, for we are endowed with consciousness and it can move us outside. This consciousness, fortunately, opens in a few people and not too often. For how could humans desire, strive to achieve their goals, fight each other, were they threatened every moment with a burst of laughter at the grotesqueness of the spectacle? For instance, if, following the advice of Gombrowicz, they take a look at a rider on a horse: an animal striding an animal, goading it to run with pieces of metal attached to its legs. How does the cavalry charge look then? Or a ball: naked males and naked females dressed in ritual rags, swaying to the sound of some silly music. Perhaps it is a ball like the one in the story by Stanislaw Vincenz about the famous mountain bandit Dobosh, who was once invited by evil spirits to a castle on the top of a mountain where gorgeously dressed ladies and gentlemen caroused. Dobosh's clever assistant noticed that the musicians from time to time reached into a bowl nearby and wet their eyes. He did the same and saw that the dancers were skeletons, the musicians devils, and the castle a desolate ruin.

In other words, suddenly he found himself outside. And we, are we not seduced by speech? Oratory, high ideological chanting, philosophies, theories—all of them grafted on excrementalities and exhalations of our bodies.

There was a writer who made an excursion outside, but his adventure proves how dangerous it is. Dean Jonathan Swift discovered that whoever once disconnects himself and watches humanity from an astronomical distance loses the ability to immerse himself again in the little joys and occupations of everyday life. When he returned from the country of the noble horses and his wife embraced him, did he not faint because of her stench? The story is, of course, well known. The island of philosophizing horses was *ou topos*, utopia, an indication of our double belonging, here, inside, and there, outside, or, if you prefer, of our split into a body imprisoned in transience and a mind soaring above it.

BE LIKE OTHERS

Wherever you lived—in the city of Pergamum at the time of the Emperor Hadrian, in Marseilles under Louis XV, or in the New Amsterdam of the colonists—be aware that you should consider yourself lucky if your life followed the pattern of life of your neighbors. If you moved, thought, felt, just as they did; and, just as they, you did what was prescribed for a given moment. If, year after year, duties and rituals became part of you, and you took a wife, brought up children, and could meet peacefully the darkening days of old age.

Think of those who were refused a blessed resemblance to their fellow men. Of those who tried hard to act correctly, so that they would be spoken of no worse than their kin, but who did not succeed in anything, for whom everything would go wrong because of some invisible flaw. And who at last for that undeserved affliction would receive the punishment of loneliness, and who did not even try then to hide their fate.

On a bench in a public park, with a paper bag from which the neck of a bottle protrudes, under the bridges of big cities, on sidewalks where the homeless keep their bundles, in a slum street with neon, waiting in front of a bar for the hour of opening, they, a nation of the excluded, whose day begins and ends with the awareness of failure. Think, how great is your luck. You did not even have to notice such as they, even though there were many nearby. Praise mediocrity and rejoice that you did not have to associate yourself with rebels. For, after all, the rebels also were bearers of disagreement with the laws of life, and of exaggerated hope, just like those who were marked in advance to fail.

A KEY

We were guests in the house of a multimillionaire and we were standing with our drinks in an inner patio, surrounded by box hedges and lawns. The host complained of his gardeners and architects. They had arranged everything wrong, and he could not keep any pets: dogs avoided the bushes and the grass, as if aware that all the greenery had been grown with chemicals and exuded a harmful vapor.

In another part of the dream, reproaches were made to our host for receiving people of suspect nationalities, swindlers and thieves, Poles, pimps, and mafiosi Italians. Yet to these he would demonstrate his superiority, very clearly, which was probably the cause of the next sequence of events, when I kicked him in the groin and eluded arrest only thanks to my strong political position.

Still in the same dream, I managed to formulate a counsel for beginning writers. There is only one big theme, a key which will open the treasury of your unrevealed and unconfessed, even to yourselves, experiences. These are the moments when you were, in one way or another, humiliated. Remember, remember only those instants sticking in you like thorns, start harrowing them, and describe them in detail. It's hard to tell what you will dig out, but that masochistic operation will bring you relief.

ANCESTORS

To tell the truth, we should not exist. We, not any collective plural, just you and me. Let us use our imaginations to visualize for a moment the circumstances and conditions of the life of our parents, then our grandparents, then great-grandparents, thus further and further back. Even if among them all there happened to be wealthy individuals or men of privilege, the stench and filth in which they lived, as that was then the rule, would have astonished us who use showers and toilets. What was even more certain was the presence among them of starvelings, for whom a piece of dry bread in pre-harvest time meant happiness. Our ancestors died like flies from epidemics, from starvation, from wars, and though children swarmed, for every twelve of them only one or two survived. And what strange tribes, what ugly snouts behind you and me, what bloody rites in honor of gods carved in the trunk of a linden tree! Back to those who are stalking through the undergrowth of a murky primeval forest with chipped stones for their only weapons, in order to split the skulls of their enemies. It would seem as if we had only parents and that's all, but those other pre-pre-predecessors exist, and with them their afflictions, manias, mental illnesses, syphilis, tuberculosis, and whatnot, and how do you know they do not continue on in you? And what was the probability that among the children of your great-great-grandparents the one survived who would beget your ancestor? And what the probability that this would repeat itself in the next generation?

Altogether, a very slim chance that we would be born in these skins, as these, not other, individuals, in whom the genes met those of the devil knows what whores and oafs. The very fact that our species survived and even multiplied beyond measure is astonishing, for it had much against it, and the primeval forest full of animals stronger than humans may serve till now as a metaphor for man's precarious situation—let us add viruses, bacteria, earthquakes, volcanic eruptions, floods, but also his own works, atomic weapons and the pollution of nature. Our species should have disappeared a long time ago, and it is still alive, incredibly resistant. That you and I happen to be part of it should be enough to give us pause for meditation.

RIVERS

"So lasting they are, the rivers!" Only think. Sources some-
where in the mountains pulsate and springs seep from a rock,
join in a stream, in the current of a river, and the river flows
through centuries, millennia. Tribes, nations pass, and the river
is still there, and yet it is not, for water does not stay the same,
only the place and the name persist, as a metaphor for a per-
manent form and changing matter. The same rivers flowed in
Europe when none of today's countries existed and no lan-
guages known to us were spoken. It is in the names of rivers
that traces of lost tribes survive. They lived, though, so long
ago that nothing is certain and scholars make guesses which to
other scholars seem unfounded. It is not even known how many
of these names come from before the Indo-European invasion,
which is estimated to have taken place two thousand to three
thousand years B.C. Our civilization poisoned river waters, and
their contamination acquires a powerful emotional meaning.
As the course of a river is a symbol of time, we are inclined to
think of a poisoned time. And yet the sources continue to gush
and we believe time will be purified one day. I am a worshipper
of flowing and would like to entrust my sins to the waters, let
them be carried to the sea.